TENNESSEE WILLIAMS

The Glass Menagerie

with commentary and notes by
STEPHEN J. BOTTOMS

MEHTUEN DRAMA INDIA

BLOOMSBURY

NEW DELHI • LONDON • OXFORD • NEW YORK • SYDNEY

Bloomsbury Publishing India Pvt. Ltd.
Second Floor, Building No. 4
DDA Complex LSC, Pocket C – 6 & 7,
Vasant Kunj, New Delhi 110070
www.bloomsbury.com

First published in India 2015

This edition first published in the United Kingdom by Methuen Publishing Ltd 2000 Reissued with additional material and a new cover design 2008
Reissued with a new cover design 2009
Reprinted 2010, 2013, 2014

The Glass Menagerie was first published in 1945 by Random House in the United States
It was first published by New Directions in the United States in 1949
This edition is based on the text published by New Directions in 1999

Methuen Drama India
An imprint of Bloomsbury Publishing Plc

Bloomsbury Publishing, London, New Delhi, New York and Sydney
A CIP catalogue record for this book is available from the British Library

For sale in the Indian subcontinent only

ISBN 978 93 84052 47 8
20 19 18 17 16 15

Printed and bound in India by Gopsons Papers Pvt. Ltd., Noida

Contents

Tennessee Williams: 1911–1983

1911 March 26. Thomas Lanier Williams born in Columbus, Mississippi, second child and first son of Cornelius Coffin Williams and Edwina Dakin Williams (sister Rose born in 1909; younger brother Dakin born 1919).

1911–18 Thomas, Rose and Edwina live with Edwina's parents in various Southern towns, including Clarksdale, Mississippi. Cornelius works as travelling salesman.

1918 Williams family moves to St Louis, Missouri, where Cornelius takes up managerial post at International Shoe Company.

1926 Owing to financial pressure, Williams family moves to cramped apartment at 6554 Enright Avenue, in downmarket University City area of St Louis. Thomas, having enrolled for one term at Soldan High School, transfers to University City High School.

1928 Williams' first published writing: short story, 'The Vengeance of Nitocris', in *Weird Tales* magazine.

1929 Stock-market crash on Wall Street ushers in the years of the Great Depression. Williams enters University of Missouri at Columbia.

1931 Owing to family financial difficulties, Williams withdraws before completing his degree. His father sends him to work at International Shoe Company.

1935 First production of a Williams one-act play, *Cairo! Shanghai! Bombay!* by Memphis Garden Players. Williams family finally moves out of Enright Avenue apartment to two-storey house on Pershing Avenue, thanks to improvements in economic climate.

1936–37 Williams studies at Washington University, St Louis.

1937 First full-length plays produced by Mummers of St Louis: *Candles to the Sun* and *The Fugitive Kind*. Rose Williams is committed to Farmington State Mental Hospital.

1937–38 Williams studies playwriting and production at University of Iowa, where he finally completes his undergraduate education. Writes *Not About Nightingales*.

1938–39 Williams wanders the US, living in various cities. Probable first homosexual experiences around this time.

1939 Wins $100 prize in play competition organised by Group Theatre of New York, for group of four plays under collective title *American Blues*. Awarded $1,000 Rockefeller grant. Short story, 'The Field of Blue Children', is published in *Story* magazine; first published writing under the name 'Tennessee Williams'.

1940 Studies in advanced playwriting seminar at New School for Social Research, New York. Tutors include John Gassner and Erwin Piscator. Writes string of one-act plays, including *The Long Goodbye*, produced at the New School in February. December – First professional production of Williams play: *Battle of Angels* opens in Boston, but is disastrously received and folds before planned Broadway transfer. (Revised as *Orpheus Descending* in 1957.)

1941–42 Lives in a variety of locations; works on short plays and stories including 'Portrait of a Girl in Glass', later to be developed into *The Glass Menagerie*.

1943 Hired as screenwriter by Metro-Goldwyn-Mayer, but is fired after initial six-month contract expires. Writing at MGM includes early draft of *Menagerie*, titled *The Gentleman Caller*. In St Louis, Rose Williams undergoes prefrontal lobotomy at consent of her mother.

1944 Wins $1,000 award for *Battle of Angels* from National Institute for Arts and Letters. One-act play *The Purification* successfully produced at Pasadena Playhouse, California. Director Margo Jones subsequently hired to assist Eddie Dowling with *The Glass Menagerie*, which premieres at the Civic Theatre, Chicago, on 26 December. Stars Laurette Taylor, Eddie Dowling, Anthony Ross, Julie Haydon; designed by Jo Mielziner.

1945 After successful run in Chicago, *The Glass Menagerie* opens to rave reviews in New York, at Playhouse Theatre on Broadway. Runs 561 performances, and wins New York Drama Critics' Circle Award, Donaldson Award and Sidney Howard Memorial Award. *You Touched Me!*, by Williams and Donald Windham, adapted from D. H. Lawrence short story, opens on Broadway in September, to tepid response. Collected short plays published as *Twenty-Seven Wagons Full of Cotton and Other Plays*.

1947 *A Streetcar Named Desire* premieres on

Broadway, directed by Elia Kazan (who becomes long-term collaborator with Williams). Play makes history by winning Pulitzer Prize for Drama, Donaldson Award, and New York Drama Critics' Circle Award (first play ever to win all three). Williams meets Frank Merlo, who becomes his companion and lover for next fourteen years.

1948 British premiere of *The Glass Menagerie*, directed by John Gielgud, with Helen Hayes as Amanda. *Summer and Smoke* premieres on Broadway. *One Arm* published (short story collection).

1950 Film version of *The Glass Menagerie* released by Warner Brothers, starring Gertrude Lawrence, Arthur Kennedy, Jane Wyman, Kirk Douglas. *The Rose Tattoo* premieres in Chicago (opens New York 1951; wins Tony Award). Novel *The Roman Spring of Mrs Stone* published.

1951 Film version of *A Streetcar Named Desire* directed by Elia Kazan. *I Rise in Flames, Cried the Phoenix* published.

1952 *Streetcar* wins National Film Critics' Circle Award. Williams is elected to the National Institute of Arts and Letters.

1953 *Camino Real* premieres on Broadway.

1954 *Hard Candy* published (short story collection).

1955 *Cat on a Hot Tin Roof* premieres on Broadway, runs 649 performances. Wins Pulitzer Prize for Drama, Donaldson Award, and New York Drama Critics' Circle Award. Film version of *The Rose Tattoo* is released.

1956 Film *Baby Doll* opens, directed by Elia Kazan. Williams' first original screenplay. Film is

condemned by Catholic Church.
1957 *Orpheus Descending* opens on Broadway. Cornelius Williams dies, aged 68.
1958 *Suddenly Last Summer* opens in off-Broadway production (double-bill with *Something Unspoken*). Film version of *Cat on a Hot Tin Roof* released.
1959 *Sweet Bird of Youth* opens on Broadway. Film version of *Suddenly Last Summer* released.
1960 *Period of Adjustment* opens on Broadway after Miami try-out. *The Fugitive Kind* (film version of *Orpheus Descending*) is released.
1961 *Night of the Iguana* opens on Broadway, wins New York Drama Critics' Circle Award. Film of *Summer and Smoke* released.
1962 *The Milk Train Doesn't Stop Here Anymore* opens at Spoleto Festival, Italy (opens New York 1963). Film version of *Sweet Bird of Youth* released.
1963 Williams' long-term lover, Frank Merlo, dies of cancer. Williams enters period of depression.
1964 Film of *Night of the Iguana* released.
1965 First major revivals of *The Glass Menagerie* in both New York and London. American production, at Brooks Atkinson Theatre, is highly acclaimed and runs for 175 performances, with Maureen Stapleton as Amanda, George Grizzard as Tom, Piper Laurie as Laura. London revival at Theatre Royal, Haymarket.
1966 *Slapstick Tragedy* opens on Broadway and flops. CBS television production of *The Glass Menagerie.*
1967 First version of *The Two-Character Play* opens in London.

1968 *The Kingdom of Earth* opens in New York. Film version of *Milk Train*, retitled *Boom!*, is released. *Seven Descents of Myrtle* produced in New York.

1969 *In the Bar of a Tokyo Hotel* opens off-Broadway. Williams awarded Gold Medal for Drama by American Academy of Arts and Letters.

1971 *Out Cry* (rewritten version of *The Two-Character Play*) opens in Chicago. Williams splits with his agent, Audrey Wood.

1972 *Small Craft Warnings* runs successfully off-Broadway, with Williams himself in the cast. Williams wins National Theatre Conference Award.

1973 ABC television version of *The Glass Menagerie*, with Katharine Hepburn as Amanda, Sam Waterston as Tom.

1974 Williams given Entertainment Hall of Fame Award and Medal of Honour for Literature from National Arts Club.

1975 Publication of Williams' *Memoirs*, and of novel *Moise and the World of Reason*. Final version of *The Two-Character Play* opens in New York. Off-Broadway revival of *The Glass Menagerie* at the Circle-in-the-Square, with Maureen Stapleton and Rip Torn.

1976 Boston try-out of *The Red Devil Battery Sign* flops and Broadway opening cancelled. *Eccentricities of Nightingale* premieres in New York. *This Is (An Entertainment)* premieres in San Francisco.

1977 *Demolition Downtown* opens in London. *Vieux Carré* opens in New York.

1978 *Crève Cœur* premieres at Spoleto Festival, North Carolina (New York 1979).

1979 Honoured at Kennedy Center, Washington DC, by President Carter.

1980 Edwina Dakin Williams dies, aged 95. *Clothes for a Summer Hotel* opens on Broadway; poorly received. Julie Haydon, *Menagerie*'s original Laura, plays Amanda in short-lived New York revival.

1981 *Something Cloudy Something Clear* opens off-Broadway. Autobiographical work dealing openly with homosexuality.

1982 *A House Not Meant to Stand* opens in Chicago.

1983 February – Tennessee Williams dies in New York hotel room, after choking on cap of pill bottle. Broadway revival of *The Glass Menagerie* opens with Jessica Tandy as Amanda. Runs 92 performances.

1985 London revival of *Menagerie* at Greenwich Theatre, with Constance Cummings as Amanda.

1987 Cineplex Odeon film version of *The Glass Menagerie*, directed by Paul Newman with Joanne Woodward as Amanda, John Malkovich as Tom.

1989 London revival of *Menagerie* at Young Vic, with Susannah York as Amanda.

1994 Roundabout Theatre mounts New York revival of *Menagerie*, with Julie Harris as Amanda and Calista Flockhart as Laura.

1995 Donmar Warehouse mounts acclaimed London revival of *Menagerie*, directed by Sam Mendes with Zoë Wanamaker as Amanda and Claire Skinner as Laura. Transfers to West End's Comedy Theatre after initial run.

1998 *Not About Nightingales* premieres, sixty years after it was written, at London's Royal National Theatre.

SYNOPSIS

The Glass Menagerie is divided into seven scenes. These are of uneven length: in production, the interval follows Scene Five, since Scenes Six and Seven are easily the longest in the play. The scenes are written in episodic form, which means that, rather than each scene simply leading directly on to the next in a single narrative trajectory, each scene (or 'episode') has its own internal narrative, largely self-contained in its action and themes. Of course, each also contributes to the development of an overarching plot, yet in several instances we are led to understand that long periods of time have elapsed between scenes: taken as a whole, the play's narrative is spread out across a large part of 1938, from winter to summer. Perhaps it is useful to think of the play as operating like a series of inter-related paintings, each one of which presents a key component in a much bigger narrative, and which together build up to create an impression – but perhaps not a conclusive understanding – of that 'whole story'. Williams shows us enough to give us a strong sense of the way that the Wingfield family operates (and indeed disintegrates), but also leaves much that is mysterious or uncertain. The reason for this approach is clear: could the 'whole story' of *any* family be told on stage in two hours?

Scene One (opening narration)

The play opens with a scene-setting narration from the

storyteller character, Tom. He addresses the audience as if he knows he is standing in a theatre, in the same time and place as the audience, and asks us to imagine ourselves into the past, the 1930s of his youth. (When the play was first produced, in 1944, it was easy for audiences to imagine Tom as a real person talking about his own family history. More than fifty years later, Tom would have to be a very old man to exist in the audience's 'present time', so instead today he seems more like a mysterious chorus figure, standing outside of time itself.) Tom briefly sketches in 'the social background of the play', referring to the Great Depression and the economic problems then facing America, and also to the Civil War taking place in Spain (1936–9). His reference to Guernica, which alludes to the merciless aerial bombing of the Spanish town of that name in April 1937, implicitly locates the action of the play after that event. His reference to St Louis, on the end of a brief list of American cities (and with a slight pause after he has mentioned it), obliquely indicates the setting for the action which is to follow.

Having alluded to the real time and real place of the story, Tom then goes on to complicate matters by stressing that what we are about to see is *not* actually 'realistic' at all. We are not going to see a photographic reproduction of his life in the 1930s, but his life as he *remembers* it. We will view the action through the lens of Tom's self-confessed nostalgia, and this is going to affect everything from the lighting of the stage to the music we hear. By stressing the way that memory can play tricks on us, Tom is implicitly warning us that we should not necessarily take everything we see at face value. We have to understand that the events we are about to see are being depicted the way Tom remembers them, rather than as some straightforward, objective reality. For example, Tom's description of the 'larger-than-life-size photograph' of his absent father, which looms over the living-room setting, seems to suggest that the size of the image has grown artificially large in his memory – thereby reflecting the length of the shadow which the father's memory still casts over the characters in the play. Tom also lets it be known that he might at times wilfully distort or manipulate the facts (as he remembers them) for the sake of dramatic or poetic effect. Referring to the gentleman caller, he tells us unashamedly that 'I am using this character . . .'. The overall effect of this opening speech is double-edged: the audience is simultaneously drawn into Tom's memory-world and – thanks to such comments – set at something of a critical distance, left to puzzle over what might be 'real' and what might be distortion or invention.

Scene One (Amanda)

Having described his father's abrupt departure 'a long time ago', Tom ends his own narration rather abruptly and we move straight into a scene from his past. His mother, Amanda, calls him in for dinner. Seconds later, though, we seem to have jumped forward into the middle of the meal, and Amanda is berating Tom for eating too hastily. This stitch in time, coming after only three lines of regular dialogue, further underlines the point that what we are seeing is conditioned by Tom's memory of what is significant. This first episode in the play is, in effect, a portrait of Amanda, but we are seeing first the way Tom remembers Amanda – calling for him to hurry to the table, nagging him about the way he eats, telling him he smokes too much. Instantly she appears as a pressure and a burden *on Tom*.

As the scene develops, however, Amanda begins to talk about her own memories of *her* youth (or rather, Tom remembers her remembering). Now she begins to be fleshed out as a character in her own right. In some ways she seems quite comic, recalling a golden age of gentility in the Deep South which must surely be her own romanticisation of the past: do we really believe, for instance, that she once had seventeen gentleman callers, or is that a statistic that is exaggerated a little further each time the story is told? Has she, likewise, romanticised the fates of her various old boyfriends (a drowning, a shooting, and so on) so that they now sound like events from some old melodrama? Amanda's memories further emphasise the theme of the past being unstable, and subject to reinvention, which Tom himself has already introduced. Towards the end of her monologue, though, we come to recognise the emotional truth underlying Amanda's romanticism: she feels that the glory of her youth was lost because of her decision to marry Tom's and Laura's father, a choice which took her away from the old Southern ways of Blue Mountain and into this cramped, modern, urban apartment. Nostalgia and regret dominate Amanda's life – or at least her life as Tom presents it in this first scene.

We are also given the impression that this scene is one which took place, with slight variations, many times over: the tale Amanda tells is apparently one that her children have heard time and again. The scene ends, however, with the focus of attention shifting slightly toward Laura: Amanda apparently wants to be able to live vicariously through her daughter, to see her receive the kind of attention from gentleman callers which she herself claims she received in her long-ago youth. Laura, however, is not the kind of girl to attract male admirers, and in the scene's final lines we glimpse briefly both her loneliness and the source of her alienation from her uncomprehending mother.

Scene Two (Laura)

The conclusion of Scene One thus sets us up for a fluid progression into Scene Two. Here, our attention is focused on Laura herself, although since she is a much quieter figure than her mother, she does not present herself through monologue as Amanda has. Laura's story is instead told more through her interaction with her mother, and we are shown a particular incident – during the winter months – in which Amanda returns home to confront Laura. Amanda has just discovered that Laura has only been pretending to attend a secretarial course at business college each day, and that in fact she has been absent from the college for the last six weeks. Laura has to face the anger and indignation of her mother, and to try to explain why she dropped out, and why she could not bring herself to tell Amanda about this earlier. She is clearly terrified by the memory of the typing course, which made her feel physically sick because she could not cope with its pressures, but she is perhaps even more afraid of her mother's disappointment in her, which is why she has been pretending that she was still taking the course.

What we see in this scene, then, are two different kinds of 'acting'. Laura attempts, rather pathetically, to keep up the illusion that she is studying: she rushes to hide her glass animals when Amanda returns home and pretends to be quietly studying her typewriter chart.

Her mother, by contrast, decides to play out her revelations as full-blown melodrama: the stage directions specify 'a bit of acting' after Amanda's first line – suggesting that she is *putting on* an air of bitter disappointment so as to emphasise her daughter's humiliation. She then goes on to play out the story of her trip to Rubicam's Business College as a blow-by-blow account in which she even mimics the voice of the woman she spoke to, so that we can imagine the whole dialogue that took place (as Amanda tells it, this was a rather terse, or even bitchy exchange). Amanda uses the story as a weapon against Laura, missing no opportunity to twist the knife by pointing out that, if Laura is not going to learn a job skill, then she has no future ('what is going to become of us?'). Laura, meanwhile, cannot stand up to her mother and responds only with inarticulate sounds of helplessness ('Oh'), and by taking refuge in trying to wind up her Victrola, an action which only infuriates her mother further.

It becomes clear during this scene that Laura has been hiding not only from her mother but from life outside the apartment. She has created an imaginary world for herself, into which she retreats whenever she can, and especially when she is placed under pressure. This imaginary world revolves around three of her personal possessions. First, there is the collection of tiny glass animals (the menagerie of the play's title) which we see her cleaning lovingly at the scene's opening. Second, there is the old Victrola record player left behind by her father, which is the ostensible source for the nostalgic, faraway music which accompanies the whole play (and which is described so carefully by Williams in his production notes). Laura's third precious possession is her high school yearbook, which she treasures chiefly because of the pictures it holds of Jim, the unrequited love of her life. In this scene, Laura plucks up courage to show her mother the yearbook, after Amanda has finally stopped ranting at her and has asked, with apparent pity, whether or not she ever 'liked some boy'. Invited to speak about something she really cares about, Laura finally finds a voice and begins to enthuse about Jim and all his exploits as 'high school hero'. It becomes clear from her comments that he barely knew her, but that she particularly treasures the few moments when she spoke with him, and the fact that he even had a nickname for her. (Jim would 'holler, "Hello, Blue Roses!"' whenever he saw her, she tells us: the hollering indicates that she only really saw him in passing at a distance.)

Laura also preserves a six-year-old newspaper clipping, presumably tucked inside the yearbook, which details Jim's engagement to Emily Meisenbach ('It says in the Personal Section', rather than 'it said', indicates that she still has the clipping with her). She seems to see his having married as marking the end of her one and only hope of ever having a happy relationship with a man, but that hope had clearly only ever been based on a dream, a longing, rather than anything more solid. Here we see the depths of Laura's isolation and lack of faith in herself, and Amanda too, seeing as if for the first time that Laura does (or at least did) dream of loving a man, resolves to help her find one to marry. This, in her view, is the only realistic alternative to the secretarial career which Laura has thrown away. Ironically then, we see that it is Laura's mention of Jim which prompts Amanda to find a 'gentleman caller' for her – a caller who, when he later appears, is in fact that same Jim.

If that seems rather too convenient a plot twist, we must remember a further underlying factor in this scene; namely, that Tom does not actually appear in it. If he was not there, how could he 'remember' these events? Perhaps what we see here is only the way Tom *imagines* that it must have taken place, based on what he learned about it afterwards, or even what Tom *wants* to have taken place, for the sake of neatness in his plot. He does not draw our attention to this point, of course, and it is not vitally important that we notice it, but if we are aware of it, this adds further to our sense that what we are seeing is a fabrication of memory and imagination.

Scene Three (opening monologues)

Tom reappears to assert his presence as narrator at the opening of Scene Three, explaining how – as winter moved into spring – Amanda's campaign to find a gentleman caller for Laura began to bring added emotional pressure to the already tense relations among the Wingfields. Amanda's preoccupation with this idea, we are told, only added further to Laura's chronic nervousness and to Tom's discomfort at home. It also apparently prompted Amanda herself to take up a telesales position to earn extra money 'to plume the bird and feather the nest' (that is, to put toward making Laura's appearance and possible dowry more appealing to prospective suitors). We next see Amanda at work making one of her telephone sales pitches, and here again her talent as a performer becomes apparent. She first gushes with sympathy for one of her friends from the D.A.R. (Daughters of the American Revolution: a respected women's organisation), and then tries to talk up the latest pulp fiction story in the *Homemaker's Companion*. Her hard-sell approach is underlined by the absurdly exaggerated claims she makes for the story as a successor to Margaret Mitchell's classic Civil War novel, *Gone With the Wind*. Comically though (and perhaps Tom's sense of irony is again apparent here), her friend finds an excuse to hang up on her in mid-sentence.

Scene Three (Tom)

Scene Three proper finally brings the focus back to Tom himself, and his sense of being trapped in his home and his job (as a clerk at a shoe factory), unable to find the time or privacy in which he can pursue his interest in literature. He dreams of becoming a writer, but Amanda even attempts to censor what he can read, banning D.H. Lawrence's novels from the house. Tom resents this, not least because he himself pays for the upkeep of the house out of his wages. Yet Amanda is still in charge of the home through sheer force of will. Tom is frustrated, powerless and penniless, and in this scene, prevented by his enraged mother from simply leaving the house as usual, he erupts into a blazing row with her. As each grows angrier, they become more hurtful towards each other, Amanda eventually accusing Tom of lying about his nocturnal habit of going to movies, and suggesting that he is really spending his nights getting drunk. Tom reacts to this with an impassioned monologue in which he desperately tries to make her understand how unhappy he is and how much he is sacrificing for her and Laura, yet she seems unwilling to listen. He therefore gives up and instead becomes blisteringly sarcastic: he too now proves himself a gifted 'actor' as he launches into a parody of what he believes she is waiting to hear, confessing to all kinds of bizarre, exaggerated nocturnal sins. Losing his head completely, he concludes by openly mocking Amanda, calling her a witch, and attempting once again to storm out of the door. In the process, he accidentally flings his coat in the direction of Laura's treasured glass menagerie, breaking something as a result. Laura, who has witnessed this whole scene, is understandably horrified, but so too is Tom himself, who stops dead in his tracks when he realises what he has done to Laura's treasures. Amanda, preoccupied with Tom's insults and oblivious to Laura, declares that she will not speak to Tom until he apologises to her, and storms out leaving her children to clear up the damage.

Although this scene seems to revolve around Tom and his struggles with his mother, it is important to note that Laura is present throughout, suffering through their fighting. Indeed, Williams specifies that she is to be lit differently and more clearly than either of the other characters: he thus creates a kind of split focus on stage, so that the audience remains strongly aware of Laura throughout the scene, again noticing her isolation even within the family. Yet it also becomes clear in this scene that there is more to Laura than helpless shyness, since the one occasion when she plucks up courage to intervene in Tom and Amanda's argument is when Tom is on the verge of swearing at his mother. This moment, echoing a similar such intervention during Scene One, demonstrates that Laura is very much aware of the need to maintain a careful emotional balance in the house in order for the family to function. She will try to intervene in the situation if Tom and Amanda are in danger of doing something they will regret. Sadly for her, though, in this scene she remains powerless to stop

Tom building himself into a rage, or his consequent damage of her treasured glass collection.

Scene Four (5 a.m.)

Scene Four depicts events in the Wingfield household early one morning in spring. In practice, though, it is really two separate scenes. The first, shorter scene takes place at 5 a.m. (the time chimed by a nearby church clock), when Tom returns home very drunk from one of his nocturnal sprees. The second begins, according to Laura, at 'nearly seven'. In between these scenes we also hear the clock striking six, Amanda's consequent calls of 'Rise and Shine!', and Tom's sleepy protests. Apparently he sleeps on for nearly an hour longer than he is supposed to. That missing hour is marked only by a few moments on stage during which the lighting increases slightly in intensity. In effect, what we as the audience witness are the moments in which Tom himself is awake (or semi-awake), which are – of course – the way he would remember these events.

The short scene at five in the morning is intriguing for the audience because it confirms for us Amanda's suspicions that Tom does not merely go to the movies at night (we can assume that no movie-theatre opens that late). Yet the mystery of what has occurred during Tom's lost hours remains unanswered: when Laura – awakened by his drunken fumbling for his doorkey – asks him where he has been, he simply explains that the movies had 'a very long program', and goes on to describe the magician's stage show which he also saw as part of the same bill. There is, of course, no particularly good reason why we should believe this story. He says the magician gave him whisky, but that could be just an embroidered cover story. Likewise, he could have found the rainbow-coloured scarf which he gives to Laura at some open-all-hours backstreet jumble shop. We might legitimately choose to believe that he did get it from 'Malvolio the Magnificent', as he claims, but the point is that neither we nor Laura have any way of knowing for sure (and since Malvolio is a character in Shakespeare's *Twelfth Night*, even that name could be a private literary joke of Tom's). What is clear, however, is the underlying emotional truth of this scene: Tom's desperation to escape the suffocating, 'nailed up coffin' of his home life has caused him to stay out all night and to lose himself in alcohol. As a result, he can catch only a couple of hours' sleep before having to go back to work. There is the unmistakable sense, as Tom climbs into bed, that something will have to give soon in this situation.

Scene Four (7 a.m.)
The later part of this scene opens with Laura pressing Tom to wake up, and to apologise to Amanda for what he said in Scene Three, as she is not speaking to him. We might conclude that this is the morning after that row took place, although it is by no means certain (perhaps there has been frosty silence in the house for days!). Moreover, Amanda's mention later in this scene of Tom having come home drunk one night, in a 'terrifying condition', seems to overlap with what we have just seen, and yet presumably refers to another, earlier occasion. These touches leave us with the impression that the situations depicted in these scenes are by no means one-off occurrences.

After waking Tom, Laura is sent out for groceries,

leaving her brother to confront Amanda. A lengthy series of stage directions indicates a sort of comic, silent-movie sequence taking place between them – all averted eye contact and awkward clearing of throats – before Tom finally plucks up the courage to apologise for calling her a witch. This acts as a kind of trigger, releasing the torrents of Amanda's pent-up emotion. If she has appeared rather falsely melodramatic at times in previous scenes, we now begin to get a deeper and more sympathetic impression of her. Although she cannot quite find it in herself to apologise for her sometimes cruel behaviour, it is clear from her explanation how much she really loves and cares for her children, and that it is *circumstances* which have made her as hard and embittered as she is. We realise here that Amanda's struggle to bring her children up and provide for them, in very difficult economic times, without the support of a husband, has made her who she is. And now it becomes clear that her continual nagging at Tom (over drinking his coffee too fast, eating a proper breakfast, staying out at night drinking, and so on) is born out of genuine, and not entirely misplaced concern for his welfare. Likewise, Amanda's insistence on discussing Laura's situation with Tom is driven by her awareness that something needs to be done for her; whereas Tom himself – however much he loves his sister – has seemed too preoccupied with his own unhappiness to think clearly about helping her. Amanda confronts him directly with this point towards the end of the scene, accusing him of thinking only about himself. This is a moment which in a way sums up the tensions between mother and son, for she is at once quite right in her criticism and overly harsh, failing to understand things from his point of view. This scene summarises, perhaps better than any other in the play, Williams' deeply humane awareness that, while an individual's behaviour might seem cruel or selfish from the outside, it may well become understandable or even sympathetic when one tries to appreciate circumstances from that individual's point of view. On several occasions in this scene, both Amanda and Tom seem simultaneously 'right' and 'wrong' in their words and actions.

A further complicating factor is that it seems Amanda and Tom are never very likely to appreciate each other's points of view fully, because they are fundamentally unable to communicate. Amanda admits that she does not know how to express to him what she feels in her heart, and the irony is that it is in this moment of helpless inarticulacy that mother and son actually seem closest: he understands her because he has had exactly the same difficulties in expressing himself. Elsewhere in the scene, though, Tom is conspicuous for his failure even to attempt to help Amanda understand him, despite her unusual openness to him. He continues in this scene to evade her questions about where he goes at night, and offers only facetious, one-line retorts to her attempts to talk about his job. Perhaps he knows that telling her where he really goes, what he really thinks, would only hurt and upset his mother more, and this is why he sidesteps her pestering. (Sure enough, in the one moment when he does speak freely, she instantly responds with a lecture on bourgeois, 'Christian' ethics.) Yet Tom, by failing to respond fully to his mother's fumbling attempts at communication, only adds further to the gulf of understanding between them. Their situation seems intractable.

Yet another subtext in the scene is, quite simply, Amanda's obvious fear for her own future. She finally confronts Tom with her knowledge that he has been in touch with the Merchant Marine, and must be thinking of running away to sea. This would deprive the family of his warehouse wage and plunge them into poverty. Amanda insists that she is not concerned for her own future, only for Laura's, but in this she is clearly being disingenuous ('I'm old and don't matter!'). Her insistence that Tom help find a potential husband for Laura is clearly motivated as much by her own concern to be provided for in old age as it is by love for Laura. Again we are aware of how the understandable instinct for self-preservation can become mixed up with the more noble motive of concern for others. For Williams, there are no easy, unambiguous explanations for people's behaviour. Similarly, when Tom finally agrees to find a gentleman caller for Laura, it seems to be driven as much by the guilt which Amanda has stirred up, and by his own desire for her to stop pestering him, as by any sense of brotherly love for his sister. Tom seems to remain justifiably sceptical that a husband is what Laura really needs, or indeed that she could attract one (a point he makes explicitly in the next scene). Yet Amanda, the bit between her teeth, plunges ahead with her campaign: after Tom has left for work, his promise made, she returns to her fundraising telesales campaign. The repetition of her sales pitch here seems like a sadly ironic touch: she disappears again behind the brittle façade of the performer, after a scene in which she has allowed herself to appear more vulnerable than at any previous point in the play.

Scene Five (Annunciation)

This scene takes place some time later, on a spring

evening warm enough for Tom to sit outside smoking on the fire escape after dinner. He is driven outside, once again, by Amanda's pestering, although on this occasion (perhaps learning from their conversation before) she seems to be making more of an effort to be constructive rather than simply nag him. She suggests that if he gave up smoking, he could afford to improve himself with a nightschool course, but Tom, dreaming of escape, is not interested in learning to be an accountant.

On the terrace, he steps out of the scene itself to address the audience as narrator once again. Accompanied by the sound of dance music, he wistfully describes his fascination with watching the goings-on in the dance hall across the alley, and – more seriously – his sense that its sensuous pleasures provided a kind of welcome distraction from the impending sense of doom which was felt that spring of 1938 by anyone paying attention to the news from Europe. Tom's newspaper headline notes that General Franco, the fascist leader, has scored another victory in the Spanish Civil War, while in his narration Tom alludes to the misguided attempts of Western leaders, like the British Prime Minister Neville Chamberlain, to appease Nazi Germany's Adolf Hitler by signing a deal in Munich which would allow Germany to annex large parts of Czechoslovakia. As Tom's last line here makes clear ('all the world was waiting for bombardments'), a second world war seemed imminent, despite Chamberlain's belief that he had secured 'peace in our time'.

The appearance of such a speech, at this juncture in the play, functions to bring an added sense of ominousness to what follows: Tom announces to Amanda, who has followed him out onto the terrace, that Laura is finally to have a gentleman caller. Although this news is delivered in one of the most playfully light-hearted exchanges between mother and son in the entire play, its location after Tom's rumours-of-war speech provides a dark counterpoint to their good humour, a sense that the news of Jim's imminent arrival might itself herald a disaster of smaller scale but of similar irreversibility.

Tom's announcement that Jim will come for dinner tomorrow night sends Amanda into a whirl of panicked preparations. Tom insists that no fuss is necessary, although he also finds amusement in his mother's predictable reaction to his news (which is perhaps partly why he drops it in so casually and at such short notice). He then responds with a kind of wry disbelief as Amanda begins to grill him with questions about every detail of Jim's background, career and appearance. She also does not let slip the chance to do a little reminiscing about her own days of receiving gentleman callers in Blue Mountain. Amanda has very fixed ideas about what to look for in a potential suitor, and it eventually emerges that the ambitious Jim is indeed eminently suitable (if with a few regrettable foibles). Tom attempts gently to remind his mother that Jim has not even met Laura yet, let alone asked for her hand in marriage, but Amanda is not to be deterred. Once again, an ironic reversal takes place here as Tom – faced with a mother so intent on pursuing her quarry that she will not admit to the problems on her doorstep – forcibly reminds her of Laura's acutely shy and withdrawn personality, which will be an obstacle to any attempt at engineering a romance for her. Tom finds himself saying to his mother almost exactly the same lines as she said to him at the end of the previous scene, when trying to remind him of his responsibility to his sister. Williams thus subtly points out the way that we can all lose sight of the obvious when blinded by our own preoccupations. Unlike his mother in the previous scene, though, Tom gives up trying to press his point home, and simply takes the familiar option of walking out. His wearily evasive explanation that he is going to the movies predictably infuriates his mother, but even this will not deter her from her path now that a gentleman caller is imminent: the scene concludes with Amanda dragging Laura out of the kitchen and onto the fire escape so that she can make a wish on the moon for happiness. It is a poignant climax to the first half of the play: Amanda is willing to draw even on the fragile sense of hope provided by the softly glowing heavens, as if this alone might provide her family with a way out of its current, self-destroying stasis.

Scene Six (opening narration)
The audience is welcomed back from the interval by Tom, who begins a lengthy narration about Jim O'Connor, the imminent gentleman caller. Jim, it emerges, not only works in the shoe warehouse with Tom, but was also at the same high school. Tom speaks wryly but also a little enviously of Jim's near-legendary status as all-round high school star, a career which contrasted sharply with his own insignificance. Yet he also notes how Jim's ambitions after high school were thwarted, apparently by the economic realities of the Depression, which have placed him on the same plane of apparent mediocrity as Tom himself. Now, they seem almost to rely on each other. Jim, Tom tells us, finds reassurance in knowing that Tom, at least, remembers

his former glories and thus, perhaps, his future potential. Yet it is also clear that Tom finds reassurance in knowing that Jim understands at least a little about him: Jim is the one person in Tom's life who seems to acknowledge and even encourage (if only lightheartedly) his ambition to be a poet.

Tom concludes his narration, however, by shifting our attention to the fact that Jim and Laura had known each other slightly at high school. He tells us that, when he invited Jim to dinner, he did not know whether or not Jim would even remember Laura when he met her. Tom also indicates that, at this time, he was unaware quite how much Jim's memory meant to Laura (he only remembers her speaking 'admiringly of his voice'). The older Tom who is narrating, knowing the results of this meeting with hindsight, does not give anything of his plot away, but clearly suggests to us – through the sense of portent in this last paragraph – that the play is now beginning to move toward events of life-changing significance.

Scene Six (preparations)

The lights come up across the stage to show us an apartment which looks far neater and more 'presentable' than it has been in the first half of the play. Amanda has 'worked like a Turk' to get it ready for the visit, and is now doing the same for Laura herself, who stands sheepishly in a new dress as Amanda fixes its hem. It is clear, however, that Laura is being made to feel very uneasy and pressurised by all the fuss her mother is making – especially when Amanda insists on artificially enlarging her bosom using powder puffs. Laura does not feel pretty or alluring, and being forced to put on a show like this only makes her still more self-conscious than usual. By stark contrast, though, the opportunity to dress up prettily is one which fills Amanda with excitement, a point which becomes very clear when she reappears, after a brief absence, in her old cotillion dress. She proceeds to 'sashay' around the room while reminiscing at length about her days as a debutante in Blue Mountain. She seems to have rediscovered her youthful vigour, and although we might suspect that her memories of those days are somewhat rose-tinted, her excitement is nonetheless entertaining and even infectious for an audience: her story about her obsession with jonquils is one of the most straightforwardly entertaining moments in the play. The fun ends quite suddenly, however, when Amanda recalls how those golden days abruptly came to a halt when she met Laura's father.

Bringing herself back to the present, Amanda notes that it is about to rain: this is an unfortunate omen for the evening which renews the sense of foreboding that Tom established earlier. That foreboding deepens further as Laura asks her mother to repeat the name of the man who is coming to dinner. She then hesitatingly reveals to her mother what we have already guessed; that this is the same Jim she knew and loved in high school. This is the last straw for her: she cannot face the pressure any longer and tells Amanda that she will not be able to meet their visitor. Amanda tells her not to be so foolish, and almost immediately the doorbell announces Tom and Jim's arrival. Ordered by her mother to answer it, Laura grows almost hysterical with terror, pleading not to be made to go, until finally Amanda commands her with such force that she meekly goes to the door (as Amanda disappears into the kitchen). Yet having opened the door and been introduced to Jim by Tom, Laura instantly turns tail and retreats to the security of her Victrola, leaving Tom and Jim to entertain themselves.

Scene Six (Jim and Tom)
Feeling very awkward with the situation in the apartment, Tom too takes his usual way out and steps out onto the fire escape to smoke. Jim opts to follow him almost immediately, rather than be left alone with only the newspaper for company, and begins goodnaturedly to lecture Tom on the self-improving benefits of taking a public speaking course – no doubt responding to Tom's obvious discomfort with 'company'. Tom, though, rejects the advice and ignores Jim's attempts to suggest that he needs to improve his performance at work. Tom finally reveals that he no longer cares how he fares at the warehouse, because he is on the point of running away to sea. In an impassioned speech, Tom explains that he is sick of watching movies, of watching life happen to other people, and that he is now determined to seize a new life for himself. Jim dismisses Tom's dreams as empty fantasy, but his uncharacteristic harshness here (he calls Tom 'you drip') perhaps suggests that the contempt he feels is really for himself, a disgust at his own failure to rise above mediocrity. Here is Tom, a nobody at high school, apparently showing more guts than he in dreaming of escape. Tom is plainly thinking of pursuing a dream wherever it takes him, no matter what the risks, whereas Jim's life – by contrast – is a model of playing safe and seeking to work one's way gradually up the career ladder.

The men's discussion is interrupted by Amanda's

rather startling arrival on the terrace – all girlish vivacity and swinging cotillion dress. Without giving the men a chance to draw breath, she launches into a chattering monologue, flirtatiously addressing Jim as if he were a gentleman caller come to call on *her*. Once again she quickly finds a way into talking about her own youth in the Deep South; once again she ends up dwelling on her own choice of husband. We begin to see a certain circularity in Amanda's train of thought here (this is the second time in the scene that a speech has ended on this subject), but more important than what she says here is our awareness of her apparently incessant need to *talk*. It seems as if this is her way of dealing with nervousness and excitement. In this respect her behaviour stands in marked contrast to that of Laura, whose crippling shyness means she cannot even bring herself to face Jim. When Amanda finally calls her in from the kitchen, where she has taken refuge, she collapses in a faint from sheer nervous exhaustion. With the strange appropriateness of a dream (or perhaps of doctored memory), a thunderstorm breaks out outside at the same instant. Tom picks his sister up and lays her down on the sofa before taking his place at the dinner table with Jim and Amanda. The scene closes with grace being said for the meal, as rain comes down outside and as the audience watches not only the diners, but Laura too, alone and terrified.

Scene Seven (Jim and Laura)
Time has passed and the meal is now finishing. Laura remains where she was. However, almost as soon as the lights have come up to reveal this tableau, they are cut out again, simulating a power blackout in the apartment.

Amanda, still flirting shamelessly with Jim, lights candles and persuades him to come into the kitchen with her to look at the fuse box. We hear their voices from offstage and watch Tom and Laura wait silently on the darkened stage, until Amanda returns having concluded that the electricity has been cut off because Tom forgot to pay the power bill. Jim knows that Tom deliberately did not pay it, in order to use the money to join the Merchant Marine (as he explained in the previous scene), but Jim opts to cover for Tom by joking about his forgetfulness. Amanda now steps back from her flirtatious hostess role (although she cannot resist one last little anecdote about her candelabrum), and none-too-subtly drags Tom to the kitchen to help wash the dishes. She thus leaves Jim alone with Laura – as she clearly had always intended to do.

Clutching the candelabrum and a glass of dandelion wine, Jim hesitantly approaches the sofa where Laura is still hiding. The simple words 'Hello there, Laura' initiate what is by far the longest dialogue sequence in the play: the encounter between Jim and Laura lasts for a full half-hour of playing time on stage. This intimate, physically static scene (that is, the stage picture remains much the same throughout, neither character moving very much) needs to be especially carefully handled in production so as not to lose the audience's attention, but when well performed it is compulsive viewing, for what we see developing during Jim and Laura's conversation is – in effect – the entire cycle of an evolving relationship. The scene goes from very nervous first contact, through a gradual building-up of Laura's confidence thanks to Jim's gently insistent attention towards her, and arrives at real mutual enjoyment of each other's company. Unfortunately for Laura, though, things then begin to fall apart, as Jim brings about unintentional damage to her most treasured glass animal – the unicorn. When he then belatedly realises that she is in love with him, he grows nervously awkward before finding a way to confess to her that he already has a steady girlfriend, Betty, to whom he is engaged to be married. Within the space of half an hour, Laura is brought out of her shell, has her most fantastic hopes built up, and then watches them vanish into nothing.

One of the most noticeable things about this scene is how genuinely decent and well-intentioned Jim seems to be. We actually know very little about him prior to their dialogue, other than what Tom has told us, and what we do know has been mostly to do with his ambitiousness and popularity. It becomes clear, though, that he has not been spoiled by his successes – or perhaps that, as he himself suggests, his humbling experiences at the warehouse have helped make him more mature and down-to-earth. He still has high hopes for himself, but his concern in this scene is not to talk about himself (as might be expected). Despite Laura's terrible shyness and initial lack of responsiveness to him, he works very hard to draw her into a real, two-way conversation. Firstly he invites her to sit with him, then to move closer into the light, and then – after talking casually to help put her at her ease a little – he questions her directly about her obvious shyness. Laura responds to his apparently genuine concern for her by plucking up the courage to ask him about his singing career, and from here it is a short step to Jim realising where he has seen her before. They begin to reminisce laughingly about high school, and although Laura's mention of her crippled foot brings about a few moments of awkward embarrassment for both of them,

Jim nevertheless tries to overcome this setback and continue the conversation by attempting to persuade her that she has no need to be so self-conscious about herself.

When the conversation turns towards memories of *The Pirates of Penzance*, the high school operetta in which Jim starred, Laura produces first her yearbook and then a copy of the show's programme. She confesses that she saw him perform 'all three times'. It would be easy for Jim to be embarrassed as he begins to realise the extent of Laura's adulation of him, but he playfully offers to sign the programme for her, six years too late, and jokes about the diminished value of his autograph. Shortly after that, Laura learns that Jim did not in fact marry – nor ever intend to marry – the girl who had announced their engagement in the personal column of the newspaper. The news that he is free of other ties, combined with the fact that Jim clearly likes her and wants to encourage her to have more confidence in herself, allows Laura to begin to fantasise that her dreams about loving Jim might just come true. (Obviously, this is not stated explicitly in the text itself, but the implication is there subtextually.) The extent of Laura's newfound willingness to open up to Jim, to allow him into her private world, is now demonstrated as she shows him her glass collection, and particularly her most loved piece – a tiny, fragile unicorn that she refers to not as 'it' but as 'he'. Despite Jim's protestations, she trusts him to hold this treasure in his hand – just as if she were trusting him to hold her heart. They joke gently about the unicorn as if it had a personality, Laura now showing a sense of wit and humour which has previously remained hidden, and which Jim has brought to the surface.

After putting the unicorn down, there is a momentary lull in the conversation, suggesting a certain awkwardness about what they could discuss next after such an intimate exchange. Jim tries to cover his unease by commenting first on the size of his shadow, then on the weather, then on the music from the Paradise Dance Hall. He leaps on the idea of having Laura dance with him, and, despite her protests, sweeps her up and helps her to dance a waltz. Here we see, in miniature, an echo of the course of their whole encounter, as she moves stiffly at first but gradually gains in confidence and enjoyment. This makes the result of their dance all the more tragic: accidentally bumping into the table where Jim had placed the unicorn, they knock it off onto the floor. Picking it up, Laura discovers that its horn has been broken off. She tries to assure Jim, who is shocked at the damage he has done, that it really does not matter that much to her, but it is clear from what we know of Laura that this is a desperately sad moment for her. Her most loved possession has been irreparably damaged. We might also speculate that this breakage is symbolic of Laura herself being irreparably hurt, either by this moment or by what follows shortly afterwards. Yet, equally, we can see an admirable strength and dignity emerge in her at this moment, as she struggles against her own grief to put Jim at ease through her gentle humour. It is almost as if she is repaying the kindness he has shown, throughout the scene, in trying to put *her* at ease.

Touched by this moment, Jim attempts to express to Laura just how special she appears to be to him. She is lost for words, but he too is unable to articulate fully, almost as if what he is feeling is inexplicable even to himself. He tries to suggest that he feels for her just what he would feel for a much-loved sister, and that he wants to aid and encourage her as he would his own sister, but seconds later the pair of them have stumbled into a passionate kiss. This is a crucial turning point, just as was the breaking of the unicorn. Jim pulls away from the kiss, cursing himself for losing control, but Laura seems simply stunned. Reduced once again to silence, she offers no response to his various attempts to return to casual conversation as if nothing had happened, and so Jim finds himself explaining, haltingly and awkwardly, that he should not have kissed her, and cannot be a boyfriend to her, because he is already engaged to be married. There are two possible readings of his actions here. One is that he really had been just foolishly lost in the moment, that the kiss meant nothing, and that he looks on Laura as he would a fragile younger sister. The second and still sadder interpretation would be that he has seen something in Laura which he loves deeply, but that – because he is already engaged – he feels he must stay faithful to Betty, despite the fact that all he can really say in praise of her is that 'in a great many ways we – get along fine'. Jim is a responsible, respectable young man who feels he must 'do the right thing' by his fiancée. Yet, according to this reading of events, that means depriving both Laura and himself of possible happiness. Fate and social custom have conspired against them both.

Still more striking than Jim's obvious awkwardness and conflicting feelings is the way in which Laura responds to this outpouring of excuses. After quietly absorbing the fact that her dream of being with him is over not only for tonight but for ever, she finds the strength and presence of mind to offer him the broken unicorn as a gift. This, she tells him, is a souvenir. The words hang in the air, conjuring an extraordinary mixture of emotional possibilities. Is she giving him a gift out of love? Is she asking him to take a small part of her with him? Is she even quietly accusing him of an act of destruction? (Is she saying, in effect, 'keep this to remember how easy it is to hurt people'?) It is impossible to tell, and Jim has no chance to ask, because the moment is shattered by Amanda's loudly unsubtle entrance bearing lemonade. Jim, Laura and the audience alike are jarred rudely out of a deeply intimate moment, and Amanda's chatter resumes as if it had never left off, except that now it seems horribly, painfully invasive and inappropriate. Amanda, of course, has no idea what she has interrupted, and when Jim tries to make his excuses and leave, she pressures him to arrange a date to come again. He explains quietly about his obligations to Betty, and now it is Amanda's turn to have her hopes reduced to dust. There is nothing left to say but the conventional pleasantries, and Jim exits as hastily as decency will permit.

Amanda, unlike Laura, is not the kind of person to accept humiliation quietly, and she calls Tom in from the kitchen to accuse him of playing a cruel joke on them all. When he realises what has happened, Tom protests his innocence, insisting he had no knowledge of Jim's engagement (a fact which Jim himself has already confirmed), but Amanda does not want to listen to him. She needs someone to blame, and Tom is the most convenient target for her final, furious outburst. She also, however, unthinkingly rubs salt into Laura's wounds by describing her as a jobless, unmarried cripple: her own previous attempts to reassure Laura that she is not crippled now seem shockingly hollow. Laura, however, has retreated to her usual silence and does not react. Tom, likewise, resorts to his usual tactics and storms out of the apartment. The family seems to be right back where it started, except that this time, Tom claims, he is not going to the movies. And, as he tells us moments later in his closing narration, he ran away for ever shortly after this fateful night. For him, Jim's visit was the straw which finally broke the camel's back.

Closing narration

Significantly, though, Tom's final speech to the audience makes no attempt to justify his leaving. He knows full well, in retrospect, that his departure – however necessary it was for his own sanity and his own hopes for future happiness – was a betrayal of his family and, most particularly, of his sister. Indeed, as he makes tragically clear to us, his escape did not mean freedom for him at all, because he is still helplessly imprisoned by a sense of guilt at having left Laura alone when she must have most needed his love and support. The bleakly poetic tone of this final narration reminds us, again, that everything we have been watching is memory, or perhaps even – in the case of Jim and Laura's scene – simply an imaginary construction of what might have happened between them. Tom's description of being haunted by memories of his sister suggests that he has spent many long, painful hours dwelling on the events of that night and on what must, or might, have occurred while he was in the kitchen with Amanda. The entire play, it seems to us now, has been an attempt on Tom's part to exorcise the ghosts of that night, and now that the play is over, there is nothing further to say. But as Laura blows out her candles for the last time, there is no guarantee that Tom has succeeded in his exorcism. Perhaps he will have to come back and perform it all over again, night after night. Perhaps he is doomed to repeat this story forever – trapped by his guilt, by his memories, and by simply not knowing what became of his mother and his sister after he deserted them.

COMMENTARY

The Glass Menagerie is often thought of as Tennessee Williams' first major play, because it was this piece that first brought serious critical and public attention to his work when, in 1945, its premiere production became the hit of the theatrical season – initially in Chicago and then in New York.* Two years later, the arrival of *A Streetcar Named Desire* confirmed Williams as a world-class playwright with a distinctive, poetic voice. It is often forgotten, however, that Williams had already written a great many plays before his success with *Menagerie*, and indeed that other, far less acclaimed works appeared on Broadway in the wake of each of his first two hits (*You Touched Me* later in 1945, and *Summer and Smoke* in 1948). Williams wrote prodigiously, and in a wide range of styles, always following his own creative instincts rather than any preconceived notion of what would make a commercial or critical success.

As a result, there was (and indeed still is) debate over the artistic merit of much of his output, some of which was misunderstood or simply dismissed during his own lifetime. This is true, particularly, of the work he produced in the last two decades of his life: after a string of successes during the 1950s, his last Broadway

* The production opened in a try-out version at Chicago's Civic Theatre on 26 December 1944, and gradually gathered press and public attention. It transferred to the Playhouse Theatre, on Broadway, in March 1945, and ran there for 561 performances.

hit, *Night of the Iguana* (1961), was followed by flop after flop until his death in 1983. Yet Williams kept writing, determined that he had something to express regardless of whether or not the commercial theatre wanted to hear it. In the 1990s, a serious reassessment of his work began in the subsidised theatre sector, with many directors believing that much of his work – and particularly his later work – had been unjustly neglected. Along with the many revivals and reassessments which resulted from this interest, an early, previously unproduced work from the late 1930s, *Not About Nightingales*, was unearthed and produced at Britain's Royal National Theatre in 1998, before finding its way to acclaim on Broadway.

All of this is relevant here because it helps us to understand the pivotal significance of *The Glass Menagerie* in Tennessee Williams' career. It was this play which plucked Williams out of the penniless obscurity in which he had lived for most of his adult life (he had just turned thirty-four when the Broadway production opened). If *Menagerie* had not proved successful for him at that time, it is possible – or even probable – that he would never have achieved widespread recognition. With this piece, Williams finally succeeded in finding a dramatic mix which made his own avowedly experimental instincts accessible to a large, popular audience – an audience which understood that this was a play quite different from what was then considered 'normal' Broadway fare, and yet was drawn in by its humour, subtlety and emotional complexity. Williams, who always remained ambivalent about the seductive nature of success (as his essay 'The Catastrophe of Success' – also printed in this volume –

indicates), had stumbled upon this winning combination of experiment and accessibility almost by accident, and it was a fine balance which he found great difficulty in striking again. To this day, *The Glass Menagerie* remains the most frequently produced of his plays, and arguably the most popular with audiences. Although *A Streetcar Named Desire* and *Cat on a Hot Tin Roof* (1955) – which both achieved a similarly fine balance of conventional and innovative elements – tend to be cited by critics as Williams' greatest achievements, *Menagerie* retains a unique appeal all its own. Moreover, when discussed, it often provokes the most intensely personal responses from Williams enthusiasts.

What, then, makes this play so peculiarly appealing? A large part of the answer to this question seems to depend, quite simply, on the fact that this is a play about a family. There are, of course, many plays about families, but few of them really take the whole family as their central focus: Arthur Miller's *Death of a Salesman* (1949), for example, is mostly concerned with the relationship between a father and elder son, with the mother and other son portrayed as little more than props to this action. *Salesman*, moreover, clearly attempts to deliver a message about the insubstantiality of the American dream of material success. Williams, by contrast, has no governing agenda in *Menagerie* other than to write as truthfully as he can about his four characters – their strengths, their weaknesses, their hopes and fears – and how they function together in the claustrophobic proximity within which he places them. 'If anyone ever wrote more shrewdly and feelingly about family politics than Williams does here,' the critic Benedict Nightingale has commented, 'I don't know him.'* That assessment pinpoints the fact that, while Williams has no 'message' to peddle, the very act of writing as honestly and even-handedly as this about the shifting power struggles and tortured love within a family situation is in itself revelatory. Partly thanks to the episodic structure of the play, which allows Williams to shift the focus of his attention slightly for each scene, we are given the opportunity to see all four characters express themselves and their individual perspectives. We are also, very importantly, given the chance to make up our own minds about these characters: Williams does not try to tell us what to think about them, or tell us that any one of them is more right or wrong, good or bad, than the others. Audience members are thus allowed the space to reflect quite personally on those aspects of the family's story which connect most closely with their own experiences. 'No one among critics or audiences could understand why this ostensibly slight play affected them so deeply,' Lyle Leverich writes of the premiere production, before pointing out that the play's concerns – though very specific in time and place – are also to some extent universal: 'What they witnessed was the tragic failure of three family members to understand one another in their intertwined love' (Leverich, p. 563 – see Further Reading).

Nowhere is the play's openness to personal interpretation and response more apparent than in relation to the character of Laura. If one had to say that the play is more 'about' any one of its characters than the others, it would probably be fair to argue that this

* From Nightingale's *Times* review of the 1995 London production of *Menagerie*. Reprinted in the *London Theatre Record*, 1995 volume, p.1283. Subsequent reviews from the same source are annotated parenthetically using the abbreviation '*LTR*'.

is, ultimately, Laura's play. It is, after all, Tom's guilt over leaving his sister which eventually turns out to be the main motive for him telling the story of the play. And yet Laura has far fewer lines than any of the other characters (including Jim, who only appears in the last two scenes). She spends long periods sitting silently on stage watching the others talk, fight and laugh, and when she does speak, it is often simply in direct response to what others have said. We have largely to *guess* at what is going on inside Laura's head, and yet it is precisely because of this that she is a figure who commands such intensely personal responses from audiences. All we really know about her is that she is very fragile and shy, and in the absence of further reliable information, we tend to see her as a mirror for our own inner shyness and fragility (or that of someone we know). Many people will claim to feel something in common with Laura, which is to say that they fill in the blanks of the character's silence with some of their own most private, sheltered emotions. Laura comes to embody the vulnerability that we all hide and suppress in order to be able to function in 'a world lit by lightning' – a world of relentless noise, competition and pressure. She also embodies, more particularly, the experience of unrequited love, of having your heart broken – even unintentionally – by someone you adored but who did not adore you back. Most of us can identify directly with that, and Williams' play succeeds in tapping right into our memories of those experiences. Perhaps, just as Tom's telling of his story seems to act as a kind of exorcism for his own tortured memories, so the play itself can facilitate a kind of emotional healing for the audience members themselves, as deeply personal feelings are brought to the surface and confronted through identification with Laura's plight.

AUTOBIOGRAPHY OR FICTION?

The Glass Menagerie was also, of course, very personal for Tennessee Williams himself. His real name was Thomas Lanier Williams, and in his youth he was always known as Tom, until he chose for himself his literary alias. An awareness of that fact instantly alerts us to the possibility that, on some level, the Tom of the play is a depiction of Tennessee himself, and that his memories and his need to exorcise them are more than merely fictional. Indeed, *Menagerie* is Williams' most blatantly autobiographical play – and this from a writer whose every work was to some degree a reflection of his own history. However, as Williams himself once remarked, if it is true that all of his work is in some way autobiographical, it is equally true that none of it is. *Menagerie* is a fiction which draws heavily on Williams' own experiences of young adulthood in St Louis, Missouri (the city in which the play itself is set), but the details of the story are also fictionalised, enhanced and rearranged in numerous ways. The events of the play are not revelations of a personal history but the component parts of a distinct, poetic vision dealing with themes of memory and loss, isolation and interdependence, to name but the most obvious. Williams clearly drew heavily on personal experiences in constructing his narrative, but was in no way limited or bound by them.

Even a cursory examination of the various biographical accounts of Tennessee Williams' life show us just how much the play owes to his own background. From the late 1920s to the mid-1930s, a period which encompassed the worst years of America's Great Depression, the Williams family lived in a small St Louis apartment (at 6544 Enright Avenue) almost identical to the one in which the play is set. In this ugly, cramped building – remembered with such lyrical disgust in Williams' opening stage directions – he learned first hand about the pettiness and degradation of lower-middle-class existence. It was also from this apartment that he could often hear the strains of music from a nearby ballroom, imaginatively recreated in the play as the Paradise Dance Hall.

Like Tom, Williams also had to listen frequently to his mother – Edwina Dakin Williams – reminisce longingly about the Deep South. The daughter of an Episcopalian minister who had had a series of parishes, she had spent most of the formative years of her youth in Tennessee, before moving even further south to Mississippi, after graduating from high school shortly after the turn of the century. Here she was able to play to the full the part of the Southern belle, as a member of one of the last generations to attempt to keep alive the traditions of the antebellum (or pre-Civil War) South.* Indeed, family accounts suggest that Edwina was known on occasion to receive thirty gentleman callers in a single day, a figure which makes Amanda Wingfield's seventeen seem quite modest in comparison.

* The American Civil War had taken place between 1861 and 1865, with the Southern states fighting for the right to break away from the USA and form their own Confederacy. The heavy defeat suffered by the Confederacy, and the South's enforced acceptance of the Union, meant that southern traditionalists shifted the battle to the field of culture instead, striving to keep alive the traditional, pre-war social customs in the face of the rapid industrialisation brought in by Northern capitalists after the war. These customs, of course, included a sharp divide between classes and races: hence Amanda Wingfield's casually unthinking references to the 'nigger' servants of her youth.

However, like Amanda, Edwina made the 'mistake' of falling in love with a travelling representative of the Cumberland Telephone and Telegraph Company, Cornelius Coffin Williams. After they were married, Edwina at first remained at home in Clarksdale, Mississippi, while Cornelius continued to travel about, and their two elder children, Rose and Thomas, were born there. (Clarksdale reappears in many works by Tennessee Williams – *The Glass Menagerie* included – under the alias 'Blue Mountain'.) Eventually, however, Cornelius's company required him to settle in St Louis, Missouri, and he moved his young family there. Neither northern nor southern, Missouri had been a free state during the Civil War. Edwina always felt like a fish out of water there, and idealised her past in the South just as does Amanda in the play.

If Amanda is clearly based on Edwina, Laura is equally clearly based on Tennessee's sister Rose. Like Laura, Rose loved to play old Victrola records, and would even teach her brother the steps to dances she knew. Like Laura, Rose once enrolled after school at Rubicam's Business College (the name in the play is unchanged) in order to learn typing and shorthand, but could not handle the pressure of the coursework. She stopped going to the classes without telling her mother, and would wander about the city until it was time to go home; events which are recreated in every detail in Scene Two of the play. Amanda's subsequent decision to have Tom find a gentleman caller for Laura from among the employers of the shoe warehouse is also based on actual events. Tennessee himself worked for a period in the soul-deadening 'celotex interior' of the Continental Shoe Company for the princely sum of sixty-five dollars a month (exactly Tom's wage in the play). His workmates there included Stanley Kowalski, whose name he was to immortalise in *A Streetcar Named Desire*. However, the boy whom he apparently did once bring home to meet Rose – Jim Connor – was actually known to him through the college fraternity of which he had been a member. In the event, it turned out that Connor already had 'strings attached' – just as Jim O'Connor has in the play.

Although much of the play's action is based on real-life events, it is also clear that Williams adapted and manipulated these details for his own purposes. For example, the episode at Rubicam's Business College and Edwina's campaign to find callers for Rose actually took place several years apart, in 1930 and 1934 respectively, rather than a few months apart. In 1930, aged twenty, Rose had in fact had no trouble attracting male visitors (whereas Laura has apparently never had any), but by twenty-four she was in danger of being 'left on the shelf'; hence her mother's campaign. This is typical of Williams' tendency carefully to rearrange actual experiences into new dramatic contexts. Thus, in the play, both Laura and Tom are said to have attended Soldan High School right up to graduation (or failure to graduate), but though Rose and Thomas did attend the actual St Louis school of that name, neither was there for more than a term, after which each moved elsewhere. Williams created a past in which both siblings attended the same school at the same time in order to lend greater emotional weight to the story of Jim's visit. Furthermore, to help give Jim and Laura's relationship a 'history' (which the real life Jim and Rose never had), Williams borrowed the story of the word 'pleurosis' being misheard as 'blue roses' from the family anecdotes of a childhood friend whose father was a surgeon with

German-speaking patients who misunderstood his English (see Leverich, pp. 87–88). Williams found a way to take what had been a private joke and give it poetic resonance, 'Blue Roses' becoming the treasured pet name Jim had for Laura.

Other appropriated stories include Jim's account of taking his fiancée on a boat-trip upriver to Alton – which came directly from Williams' own memory of doing just that with an old girlfriend (see Leverich, p. 82). However, perhaps the most significant such 'borrowing' is the image of the glass menagerie itself, which – in real life – seems to have belonged not to Rose but to Mrs Maggie Wingfield, a resident of Clarksdale during Tennessee's childhood years. Mrs Wingfield, who was obviously the source for the name of the family in *Menagerie*, used to keep her collection of glass animals on display in her front window. This fact, discovered by Williams' authorised biographer Lyle Leverich, contradicts Williams' own story – sometimes told in interviews – that Rose had indeed kept glass animals, and that he had helped add to her collection. As Leverich points out, Williams was a notorious fabricator of such personal stories – 'the dramatist dramatizing himself' (Leverich, p. xxiv). According to Rose and Thomas's younger brother, Dakin (who has no equivalent in *Menagerie*), Rose had some glass ornaments, but 'just two or three pieces . . . very cheap little things, probably purchased at Woolworth's'.* Williams seems to have extrapolated from this small detail, marrying it with the memory of Mrs Wingfield's window, to create a symbolic representation of (as he

* Quoted on p. xi of Robert Bray's Introduction to *The Glass Menagerie*, published by New Directions 1999.

himself put it) 'the fragile, delicate ties that must be broken, that you inevitably break, when you try to fulfil yourself' (quoted Devlin, p. 10).

The danger of causing damage in the process of trying to fulfil yourself is further emphasised in the play's narrative by virtue of another notable deviation from Williams' own family history. In *Menagerie*, Tom's father – the 'telephone man who fell in love with long distance' – has long since abandoned his family, leaving them to the un-tender mercy of fate in order to follow his own dreams. In real life, however, Cornelius Williams traded his telephone job for one with a shoe company (which is why young Thomas was able to find work with them), and stayed for the rest of his life in St Louis. He never did leave his family, even though he and his wife were constantly fighting – at considerable cost to the emotional stability of their children. Williams, by effectively rewriting his family's history as if his father had left them, achieves several dramatic purposes. For one thing, he is able to concentrate more tightly on depicting the remaining three members of the Wingfield family, who are each haunted in different ways by the absence of the father figure. For another, he is able to render the father as a mysteriously romantic figure, a roamer of the world, rather than the stuffily unimaginative working man that Cornelius seems to have been. Tom thus has a father figure whom he can aspire to emulate – and yet at the same time, the father's selfish desertion of his family has entrapped Tom more tightly than Williams himself ever was. Tom has to be the main breadwinner for the family, and his own struggle over whether or not to leave thus has far greater consequences than it actually did for Williams. His mother and sister will be deprived of an income by his departure, and Tom himself will thus inevitably be haunted by guilt at leaving them.

Of all the play's rearrangements of historical fact, arguably the most telling is Williams' decision to locate the dramatic action very specifically around 1937 and 1938. These years are clearly alluded to by Tom's various oblique narratorial references to the bombing of Guernica, the Spanish Civil War, and Neville Chamberlain's attempts to appease Hitler. However, the period of Williams family history which the play draws on was actually much earlier in the decade (around 1932–4). By 1938, the Williamses had moved out of Enright Avenue into a better home, Tennessee was at university in Iowa, and Rose had been committed to a sanatorium for the mentally unstable. The decision to locate the play in this year suggests two motives on Williams' part, the one obvious and the other far more private. Clearly, there is a wish to relate the events of the play to the broader historical realities of 1938, with the sense of foreboding and the threat of war which seemed to be in the air at that time: Williams wanted to parallel the domestic crisis of the play with far greater crises in the world at large, creating an interwoven narrative of public and private calamity. Moreover, as Christopher Bigsby has pointed out, the allusion to Chamberlain – the British Prime Minister who thought he had secured 'peace in our time' by dealing with Hitler – 'is an invitation to read the events of the play ironically.' With historical hindsight and distance, we see that, in their own ways, each of Williams' characters is as guilty as Chamberlain of blinding himself or herself to the stark realities of their situation, and of indulging 'the desire to live with comforting fictions, rather than confront brutal truths, a doomed and ultimately deadly strategy' (Bigsby, 1997, p. 35).

On a still more personal level, the choice of 1937–8 also perhaps implies that Williams is attempting to deal, in his own allusive way, with the greatest tragedy of his family life – Rose's descent into schizophrenia. It was this event, more than any other, which troubled Williams for the rest of his life, not only because of his own helplessness to do anything about it, but because of a sense of guilt: he himself had been too preoccupied at this period – in trying to complete his stop-start university career and to find publishers for his writing – to be of much assistance to Rose at the time when she most needed his love and help. In subsequent years, Williams repeatedly attempted to exorcise the memory of his sister's decline through his writing, and it can be no mere coincidence that Tom Wingfield's abandoning of his helpless, shy sister to face the future alone shares exactly the same historical timetable as Tennessee Williams' failure to prevent his schizophrenic sister being committed to a sanatorium. (Rose was to remain institutionalised for the rest of her long life.)

The Glass Menagerie, then, can be read on one level as an attempt to find a way of dramatising the undramatisable. Not wishing to humiliate his beloved sister further by depicting Laura as insane, Williams imaginatively translated the memories of Rose's decline into a different, quieter kind of tragedy. The depiction of Laura's shyness and vulnerability – of the shattering of her tiny unicorn and of her fragile hopes for love – stands in as a kind of personal metaphor for the still more delicate state of Rose's mind. (Laura's crippled leg is also, of course, indicative of her fundamental difference and isolation from the rest of the world.) Crucially, though, Laura's situation is also far more comprehensible to an audience than is actual madness: we can sympathise with her as a person with acute emotional difficulties, whereas a schizophrenic character on stage would inevitably be viewed as something frighteningly alien to most people's experience. By hitting on the story of the gentleman caller, Williams found a way not only to face his own family's demons but to translate them into terms which seem universally accessible and applicable. That, surely, is a hallmark of great writing.

EARLIER VERSIONS

An examination of Williams' various writings in the years preceding the appearance of *The Glass Menagerie* demonstrates that he struggled long and hard to find a satisfactory way of translating his sister's story into fictional terms. An early, unpublished one-act play titled *If You Breathe, It Breaks* tells the story of Mrs Wingfield and her *three* children (a girl and two boys), and focuses on the daughter's love for her glass menagerie and her mother's attempts to find her a gentleman caller. Similarly, a short story titled 'Portrait of a Girl in Glass' tells a tale almost identical to the one in *Menagerie*: many lines which eventually appeared in the play were first used here, and the closing paragraphs were adapted with little alteration to become Tom's closing speech. One noticeable difference between these early treatments of the story and *Menagerie* itself, however, is that the sketches actually give us more information about 'Laura' – her personality and character – than does the play. In *If You Breathe, It Breaks*, for instance, the daughter rejects her mother's attempts to find her a caller, saying that she prefers to be a 'front porch girl' and watch boys go by without them coming to see her. In 'Portrait of a Girl in Glass', Jim comes to call and Laura is let down just as in the play, but she seems eerily calm and unaffected by his revelation about his fiancée Betty, commenting simply that 'People in love take everything for granted' (Williams, 1967, p. 111). This and other moments in the story suggest that this Laura is rather otherworldly, or perhaps even a little simple. She asks at one point, for example, whether real stars actually have five points like the ones on Christmas trees. The narration also describes her fascination with a romantic novel called *Freckles*, which she reads parts of over and over again, apparently because she is strangely in love with the story's hero. (This is the equivalent of *Menagerie*'s focus on Laura's yearbook and on the pictures of Jim it contains. In the last scene of *Menagerie*, Laura even refers to Jim as 'Freckles', a hangover from the earlier story.) Such touches, however endearing, also make the Laura of the story version seem more than a little odd. Perhaps they were quite faithful to Williams' experience of his sister's own oddness, but he seems to have realised that, by having Laura say less – thus making her less odd and more mysteriously shy – the play would be more profoundly affective for an audience.

Biographical accounts indicate that Rose herself was in fact anything *but* quiet and restrained. Though undoubtedly very vulnerable, she apparently 'looked and talked' very much like her mother – that is, she would chatter away incessantly just as Amanda does in the play (Leverich, p. 77). As a young woman, she had no shortage of young men wishing to date her, and she recorded lists of them in her journal, but none seems to have shown sustained interest – partly, it seems, because of her nervous chattering. By twenty-four, an unmarried virgin, she was growing desperate enough that she even sexually propositioned one of her dates (a colleague of Thomas's from the shoe company, in fact). At the time, this was an unforgiveable breach of social customs: according to their brother Dakin, Thomas was sufficiently shocked by Rose's actions to corner her at home and tell her, loudly, than she disgusted him (see Leverich, p. 142). Given this information, it is perhaps not surprising to discover that, in the years prior to writing *The Glass Menagerie*, Williams created several short pieces which seem to allude to the more unsettling, sexually provocative or taboo-breaking side of Rose's behaviour and incipient schizophrenia. A short story entitled *The Dark Room* (1940), for example, depicts an Italian mother explaining to a social worker that her 'crazy' daughter never comes out of her permanently darkened bedroom. Eventually she reveals that the girl is regularly visited in the dark by an ex-boyfriend, and that as a result she is pregnant. This is a bizarre, grotesquely funny little piece haunted by the implications of madness.

Two other short plays deal more seriously with sexually provocative young women perceived from their brother's point of view. *The Long Goodbye* (1940) depicts a young man sitting in the same apartment as *Menagerie* is set in, watching removal men take away the furniture and reminiscing about his sister, whom he sees as if in a dream. Some unnamed fate seems to have befallen her, as a result of which she has lost all self-control: 'I used to have high hopes for you, Myra. But not any more. You're goin' down the toboggan like a greased pig. Take a look at yourself in the mirror. [You look] like a whore, a cheap one' (Williams, 1945, p.

176). *The Purification* (1940) – a strangely poetic one-act fable which seems heavily influenced by Lorca's *Blood Wedding* – also depicts a young man conjuring up his now vanished sister from memory, but here the girl's loss is lamented in poetry. The language strongly suggests that Williams was thinking of Rose's madness when he wrote this piece: 'For nothing contains you now, / no, nothing contains you, / lost little girl, my sister, / not even those – little – blue veins / that carried the light to your temples' (Williams, 1945, pp. 59–60). The twist in this play is that the young man seems to have had an incestuous affair with his sister, a crime for which he finally decides to take his own life. Williams was to comment in later years that his relationship with Rose had indeed bordered on a kind of sexless incest – that their attachment to each other was the deepest one in either's life, and 'perhaps very pertinent to our withdrawal from extrafamiliar attachments' (quoted Leverich, p. 142).

For many, the most touching of these early one-act plays is *This Property is Condemned*, in which a young boy named (again) Tom encounters a girl named Willie on a deserted railway embankment. Willie, Williams tells us in his stage directions, 'is a remarkable apparition . . . dressed in outrageous cast-off finery. . . . There is something ineluctably childlike and innocent in her appearance despite the make-up. She laughs frequently and wildly with a sort of ferocious, tragic abandon' (Williams, 1945, p. 197). This seems to be his most direct attempt to dramatise, in metaphoric terms, his sister's schizophrenic condition, and the result is an eerily affectionate portrait of someone who exists completely outside the normal human world. Willie talks wildly about how she is now homeless, cast out of the house in which she grew up, which now bears a sign, 'This Property is Condemned'. The label seems to apply as much to the character as to the building.

An analysis of these various short plays leads to the necessary conclusion that the character of Laura in *The Glass Menagerie* is not, as some commentators have suggested, simply an attempt to dramatise Rose straightforwardly, as Williams remembered her. Rather, Laura is just one manifestation of Williams' many, varied attempts to exorcise his sister's memory. Still other, later variations on the same theme include Cathy in *Suddenly Last Summer* (1958), who is held in a mental hospital and is in danger of being lobotomised – as was Rose – if she does not stop 'babbling'. Laura is in fact one of the quietest and most seemingly sane of Williams' many troubled young women, and the one with whom – as has been noted – audiences seem most able to empathise. One might even argue that Williams himself seems to understand more about Laura than he does about some of his other young female characters. If that is the case, it might well be because he – like many audience members after him – was able to project something of his *own* vulnerability and shyness onto this strangely quiet character.

Indeed, the available evidence suggests that Laura is based as much on the young Tennessee as she is on Rose. Most notably, the entire scenario of her tragically unrequited love for Jim is one which draws directly on Williams' adoration of Hazel Kramer, rather than on any infatuation of Rose's. Williams and Hazel were inseparable friends throughout most of their teenage years, and he was apparently convinced that the two of them would eventually marry and start a family. This, obviously, was before he had come to terms with his homosexuality, but even in later years Williams would describe Hazel as 'the great extra-familial love of my life' (quoted Leverich, p. 72). Hazel did not, however, feel the same way about him. Instead she met and fell in love with Ed Meisenbach, who was taller and much better looking than young Thomas, and the two of them eventually married. According to his biographers, it took Williams years to come to terms with Hazel's 'betrayal', years during which he was perceived by many as acutely shy and withdrawn. Understandably then, in *The Glass Menagerie*, Williams seems to be attempting an exorcism of these events too, at the same time as exploring his sense of guilt and responsibility in regard to Rose. With the sexes reversed, Jim O'Connor is as much Hazel Kramer as he is Jim Connor the fraternity man, and Ed Meisenbach is even worked mischievously into the play as 'Emily Meisenbach', the 'kraut-head' whom Jim was supposedly due to marry after high school. Given such information, one might speculate that the closeness of the relationship between Tom and Laura can be interpreted as reflecting the interdependence shared by two parts of the same psyche – with Tom as the controlled, ironic, public voice of the poet, and Laura as his private loneliness and vulnerability (a contrast of the 'masculine' and 'feminine' sides of one self?). But perhaps that would be to venture too far into the realms of psychoanalysis. The real interest of the play, after all, lies not in any window it opens to the writer's mind, but in the way that an *audience* can connect these characters with feelings and experiences of their own.

THEATRICAL MAGIC

The deft touch with which Williams rewrote and restructured his private family history to create a more universally accessible narrative was mirrored, very importantly, by the similarly free-handed approach he took in rewriting the rulebook of theatrical convention. Considered in relation to the staid, naturalistic fare which was standard in the American theatre in the 1940s, *The Glass Menagerie* constituted a minor revolution of stylistic innovation, and the play's originality in that time helps to explain why, in many ways, it still seems so fresh today, more than half a century later. 'In this play,' the *New York Times* critic Clive Barnes commented when reviewing the 1975 Broadway revival, 'there was once a new dawn for the American theatre. And, naturally, dawns always survive' (quoted Arnott, pp. 22–3).

That new dawn, it should be noted, had been preceded by a false dawn or two. Williams, always the experimentalist, had pushed his instinct for theatricality rather too far in writing what became his first full-length, professionally produced play, *Battle of Angels*. This complex allegory of good, evil and the struggles of the creative spirit proved too bewildering for audiences when first mounted in Boston in 1940, and the production was cancelled before its intended move to Broadway. Part of the problem had been the play's over-reliance on elaborate stage effects which created a minefield of possible technical hitches (the cue sheet reportedly called for 'endless sound effects, drums, guns, lightning and thunder, offstage pinball machines, wind, rain, guitars, songs, "hound-dawgs" and musical noises': quoted Leverich, p. 391). Indeed, on one night of the short-lived run, a pyrotechnic device almost torched the audience. Williams had to wait a full four years before *The Glass Menagerie* gave him a second chance at mainstream recognition, and in this play he applied the painful lessons of *Battle of Angels* by creating a far subtler, less bombastic piece which would stand or fall on the quality of the writing and acting rather than on the efficiency of the stage management.

The primary innovation of *Menagerie* lay in its very simplicity. Williams' notebooks for the period leading up to his writing of the play include an important meditation on his struggle to find a new working method. Most conventionally realistic theatre, he believed, was dull and prosaic, and his concern was to create a kind of stage poetry, which had accounted for the overreaching ambition of *Battle of Angels*. He had concluded, however, that he needed to seek 'apocalypse without delirium', by exploring muted understatement rather than elaborate spectacle: 'I have evolved a new method which in my own particular case may turn out to be a solution. I call it the "sculptural drama". . . . I visualize it as a reduced mobility on stage, the forming of statuesque attitudes or tableaux, something resembling a restrained type of dance, with motions honed down to only the essential or significant' (quoted Leverich, p. 446). It was from this principle that Williams derived the episodic structure for *The Glass Menagerie*: rather than adhering to the then-conventional practice of presenting a play's action in two or three extended acts, he broke his narrative down into seven scenes, each of which could serve to depict a distilled, 'sculptural' image of a situation, a relational dynamic between characters. These scenes rarely call for much physical action, and to prevent them becoming merely dully static, great precision is required from directors in creating on stage the kind of moving portraiture which Williams calls for, so as to encapsulate visually the emotional circumstances of each scene. Some of his stage directions help to emphasise this point explicitly. At the beginning of Scene Five, for example, he writes of Amanda and Laura 'removing dishes from the table in the dining room . . . their movements formalized almost as a dance or ritual, their moving forms as pale and silent as moths' (p. 38). At the end of Scene Seven, Amanda is described as sitting with Laura in a silent tableau in which the only movements are her 'slow and graceful, almost dancelike [gestures], as she comforts her daughter' (p. 96).

The charged stillness and deliberate understatement of the play helps to focus the audience's attention on the subtleties of the immediate moment. The forward narrative thrust of most conventional, realistic drama is thus suspended – at least partially – and we are enabled to find a heightened awareness of both the visual presence and emotional undercurrents of the scene at hand. When *Menagerie* first appeared, this technique caused some bewilderment among critics, who were unable to account for the strange power of a play whose plot seemed so simple and even uneventful: 'The lack of action in *The Glass Menagerie* is a bit baffling at first,' noted the *New York Herald Tribune*, 'but it becomes of no consequence as one gets to know the family.'* The process of 'getting to know' the family is assisted greatly by the peculiar intimacy created by the play's relative stillness. 'Be prepared to listen and not cough,' *New York Daily News* critic John Chapman warned his readers in 1945, 'else everybody but [Jim, played by Anthony] Ross will be almost inaudible in the back of

* This quotation – along with all subsequent quotations from reviews of the 1945 New York premiere – is taken from material held in the *Glass Menagerie* press clippings folder at New York Public Library's Billy Rose Theatre Collection. Clippings are unpaginated.

the house. But I would not have it otherwise. A higher key might dispel the enchantment.' As Chapman implies, the quietness was not a result of flawed performances, but of the play itself, which needs to be played so delicately. The extended tableau of Scene Seven, in particular, in which Jim and Laura barely move from their seats on the floor around the candelabrum, has to create the illusion of being a deeply private conversation between two people sitting only inches away from each other. The scene is still frequently described by reviewers as both the highlight of the play and the point at which audiences are held in a kind of rapt silence, as they strain to hear a conversation which must necessarily be pitched in as hushed a tone as the theatre's physical size will permit.

In short, then, Williams' concern in writing *The Glass Menagerie* was to avoid the usual, mundane trappings of conventional stage realism (a manner in which, unfortunately, it is often presented), and instead arrive at a kind of heightened, intensified emotional reality through the play's use of tight focus and 'sculptural' stillness. As he says in the production notes preceding the published text, his concern is not with creating the 'photographic likeness' of a family's life, in a 'straight realistic play with its genuine Frigidaire and authentic ice-cubes', but with achieving 'a more penetrating and vivid expression of things as they are'. As if to trumpet this point from the very start, Tom declares in his opening monologue that the play 'is not realistic': rather, it attempts to evoke the hazy atmosphere of memory, and to achieve this, Tom explains, it uses dim, 'sentimental' lighting and background music to underscore scenes (common in cinema but not theatre). Technical stage devices are thus employed in a far subtler but no less significant way than they were in *Battle of Angels*. As Williams stresses in his production notes, the lighting and music are no mere appendages to the play but an integral part of his concern to create 'a new, plastic theatre' – by which he means a theatre that provides a three-dimensional sensory experience, as opposed to being primarily verbal or literary.

In America in the mid-1940s, Williams' staging ideas were highly unusual, but their successful employment in a play which proved so popular meant that *Menagerie* became extremely influential. The use of evocative music, atmospheric lighting and semi-transparent sets to create a heightened, even dream-like, new form of stage realism – which became known internationally, for a time, as 'the American Style' – was first seen in *Menagerie*, and then subsequently developed in other Williams plays such as *A Streetcar Named Desire*, and by other playwrights like Arthur Miller, who freely acknowledges the profound influence of Williams' work on the development of his own ideas for *Death of a Salesman*. One of the key staging devices in all these works was the use of gauze scenery, which when lit from the front can create the illusion of a solid wall, but which can then vanish almost completely when lit from behind. Williams made explicit use of this device in writing the stage directions for *Menagerie*, so that scenes behind the gauze could appear or dissolve magically, as they might in one's memory. Jo Mielziner, the legendary American set and lighting designer who worked on the premiere productions of all Williams' and Miller's most famous plays, once stated that, if Williams 'had written plays in the days before the technical development of translucent and transparent scenery, I believe he would have invented it.' Such devices, Mielziner stressed, 'were not just another stage trick' when used by Williams, but 'a true reflection of the contemporary playwright's interest in – and at times obsession with – the exploration of the inner man' (quoted Bigbsy, 1984, pp. 49–50).

That phrase 'the inner man' was a familiar one among artists of the first half of the twentieth century, not least because of the emergence – firstly in Germany and then, in different forms, elsewhere – of 'expressionism'. This was an aesthetic approach used in theatre, film and painting, which involved a rejection of the everyday surfaces of realism in favour of nightmarish imagery suggesting an outward 'expression' of the 'inner life' of either the artist or of the drama's protagonist. Typically, expressionist works were characterised by the use of heavily symbolic settings, stark black and white lighting, looming shadows, and so forth, to evoke a sense of inner, psychic turmoil (or *angst*, to use the German word). Williams was exposed to such ideas early on in his artistic formation (it is known, for example, that his high school mounted a production of Eugene O'Neill's expressionist play *The Hairy Ape* in 1931), and they seem to have been very important to him: in his production notes for *Menagerie* he refers to 'expressionism and all other unconventional techniques in drama' as helping inspire his concern to create a 'new plastic theatre'. *Menagerie* itself can be seen as expressionist insofar that it explores Tom's inner turmoil by depicting his memories – obviously an 'expression' of his inner mind – with the help of appropriately 'dreamlike' lighting and sound.

However, this is not an expressionist play *per se*, any more than it is a straightforwardly realistic one. For while expressionism would normally assume a tight, central focus on the struggles of the central character (as is the case, for instance, with *The Hairy Ape*), Tom is in many ways the character *least* central to the play's narrative action (which focuses on Amanda's attempts to find a gentleman caller for Laura, and the results of the caller's visit). Moreover, in Scene Three, at the point when Tom is having his most impassioned row with his mother, Williams specifies that Laura is to be lit more clearly than either of them, as if her reactions to the fight should be the real centre of attention. This is a good example of Williams' repeated use in the play of a kind of split focus effect, whereby the audience's attention is drawn in two directions at once, allowing a choice of what to look at. This strategy, as the critic David Savran has astutely pointed out, is antithetical to expressionism, and seems to have more in common with surrealism (see Savran, pp. 94–6). This was another school of modernist aesthetics which was concerned less with the idea of expressing a central, governing consciousness than with the way that the workings of the subconscious mind – experienced through dreams and the spontaneous connections of memory – can seem both entirely irrational and strangely appropriate, producing images that are laterally linked by some hidden, subliminal logic. One need only look at the paintings of René Magritte or Salvador Dali to see how multiple images or contradictory ideas can co-exist in the same pictorial space, so as to create not a centrally focused image but a kind of dream landscape.

The clearest indication of *The Glass Menagerie*'s 'surrealist' side is Williams' directions for the use of magic lantern slides during the performance of the play; he suggests various captions and images which are to be projected onto a section of the stage set's (semi-transparent) walls. Clearly this device extends his use of split focus, as the audience's attention will sometimes be drawn away from the actors to the projections, but for this very reason Williams' suggestions for projections are almost always ignored by producers. Eddie Dowling, directing the premiere production, dispensed with them because he believed they were too strange and unwieldy, and although Williams still insisted on having them included in the published script, it has often been assumed that Dowling was correct, and that the author had not really thought his ideas through properly. Some critics have even suggested that Williams' interest in this device represented a misguided attempt to borrow from the German political theatre of Erwin Piscator and Bertolt Brecht. Williams had had personal experience, in the early 1940s, of working with Piscator at New York's New School for Social Research, but he came to despise Piscator and his methods. Although he was perhaps inspired by the German director's use of film sequences and titles in his plays, his own interest in such devices had very little in common with Piscator's attempts to drum a political message into his audiences by using, for instance, documentary film footage. Rather, Williams' suggestions for his magic lantern slides indicate an extension of his concern for the creation of a highly atmospheric theatrical experience.

Magic lanterns are an early form of slide projection which produce quite hazy, unfixed images. Playing on this quality, Williams outlines a series of titles and images which suggest an attempt to evoke something of the evocative, illogical logic of dreams, rather than the political didacticism of Piscator. For example, the very first projection, in Scene One, is 'Ou sont les neiges', which is part of a famous line by the French poet

Villon: 'Ou sont les neiges d'antan?' The phrase translates as 'Where are the snows of yesteryear?', and for those familiar with it, it would automatically conjure a certain sense of nostalgia, as it does in its original context. Even for those unfamiliar with the source (or even with French), there is an oddly evocative feel to the phrase. Williams is using it as a kind of shorthand means to generate in his audience the kind of wistful emotions which are associated with nostalgic remembrance. And yet at the same time, his fragmenting of the quote, and its repetition later in the same scene, in its entirety, creates a strange sense of disjuncture: the phrase seems oddly broken, but recurs insistently, just as – in dreams – words sometimes nag at us which seem both obscure and eerily significant.

A similar use of repetition occurs in Scene Two. At the start of the scene, an image of blue roses is projected on the screen. Blue roses do not, of course, exist in real life, and the projection of the image is bound to provoke questions for audiences because it precedes any mention of blue roses in the dialogue itself (Laura explains later in the scene that this was Jim's nickname for her in high school). However, when the words are eventually mentioned, the spectator's mind is likely to connect back to the floating, poetic image of blue roses seen previously. Williams thus creates a strange, elliptical link between present and past moments, looping backwards in time rather than obeying the usual, logical linearity of dramatic narrative.

Throughout the play, the use of projections operates in suggestive ways like this, opening up strange connections and resonances rather than making specific, definable points. Titles are also used to provide a kind of ironic commentary on the dramatic action – as for instance when Jim informs Amanda that he already has a steady girlfriend. A caption reading 'the sky falls' accompanies Amanda's stunned pause, underlining just how much this means to her in a manner which is both mischievously witty and oddly moving. It should be noted that not all of Williams' projection ideas are as telling as this, partly because he never had the chance to see them 'road-tested' in production and so amend the text appropriately. He does, however, specify that productions should experiment with and extrapolate from his suggestions. The common decision to dismiss the projections as an inappropriate appendage to the action is unfortunate, because a whole dimension of Williams' conception for the play is thus lost. Even audiences of the acclaimed London production of 1995 (which experimented with staging in various innovative ways) only saw a watered-down version of the projection idea: the director Sam Mendes opted to use title captions at the beginning of each scene (some of them different from those in the script), but not to try out any of the other phrases or images suggested by Williams.

It is sometimes possible, however, in smaller-scale productions, to see all Williams' ideas put into practice. In the interests of seeing what might happen if the projection device were given a chance, I myself chose to direct a production in 1999 in which the projections were an integral part of the show. Instead of a magic lantern, we used modern video technology to create fluid, dream-like image sequences inspired by Williams' suggestions. Audience reactions to the production made it clear that we had successfully disproved the conventional assumption that the projections would distract from, rather than enhance, the actors' performance of the dialogue. The critic for Glasgow's *Herald* newspaper commented that the production had brought 'yet another layer to an already multi-faceted play, without detracting from the vital fragility that is the drama's core'. For me, that judgement demonstrates that Williams knew exactly what he was doing in his suggestions for the play's staging. *Menagerie* draws on and hybridises elements of realism, expressionism and surrealism to create what is still – more than fifty years on – a highly original theatrical experience.

PLAYING THE ROLES

As should by now be clear, *The Glass Menagerie* has to be seen in production in order for one to gain a full impression of Williams' vision. The play as written is simply the blueprint for a visual, sculptural, musical event, a fully conceived example of 'a new plastic theatre'. Simply to read the words on the page is akin to reading the score of a concerto without actually hearing it. That said, it should also be stressed that the successful presentation of *The Glass Menagerie*'s 'vital fragility' on stage depends, above all, on the work of the actors. No amount of inventiveness in direction or design will help a production if the characters are not presented persuasively.

To an extent, of course, that is true of any play, but it is especially true of a piece requiring such restrained understatement in its performance. *Menagerie* calls for a uniformly strong, ensemble cast (as opposed to a cast dominated by one or two stars), in which each actor is able to make apparent the many different sides of his or her character. Williams' notion of a 'sculptural' drama is useful in underlining the fact that this play operates to present each character from a number of different perspectives – almost as if the audience were moving around a three-dimensional sculpture to gain a complete picture of it. Viewed from one angle, for example, Amanda might appear to be an oppressive, selfish monster of a mother, yet from another she seems deeply caring. The key to any production of this play lies in the actors' ability to create the kind of heart-rendingly human portraits which allow us to understand and even sympathise with each character, as well as seeing clearly his or her flaws and mistakes. Ultimately, what makes *The Glass Menagerie* so moving is that it presents neither villains nor victims, but four characters who are all seeking, in their own ways, to 'do the right thing'. The desperate irony of the situation is that their seeking – so often at cross-purposes – leads them inexorably to create their own small tragedy.

Amanda

Amanda is the most obviously complex and multi-faceted of these characters, and Williams acknowledges as much in his initial character notes. His description of 'a little woman of great but confused vitality' immediately indicates some of her contradictions, as does his note that 'there is much to admire in Amanda, and as much to love and pity as to laugh at'. In Amanda, Williams presents us, unapologetically, with a detailed portrait of his own mother, Edwina Dakin Williams. His own conflicted feelings toward a woman he both adored and resented are readily apparent here. Whereas all the other characters in *Menagerie* are – as has been noted – creatively adapted from their real-life counterparts, the biographical evidence suggests that

Amanda's characterisation represents a fairly direct attempt on Williams' part to portray Edwina as he saw her, in all her complexity. Edwina herself often denied any connection to the character, but at other times would reportedly play up the link for her own benefit – a pattern of contradiction which would be plausible coming from Amanda herself. Certainly almost every detail of the characterisation is consistent with Amanda's real life model – from her incessant chattering to her moments of desolation, from her romantic attachment to the old South to her discomfort in St Louis, from her loudly voiced dissatisfaction with her husband to her reminiscences about her one true lost love (Duncan J. Fitzhugh in the play; John Singleton in real life: see Leverich, p. 31). According to his brother Dakin, Williams' depiction of Amanda was so true to life that Edwina could have sued him for plagiarism: he claims that not only turns of phrase but entire speeches (such as Amanda's opening monologue about not eating too fast) were lifted almost verbatim from Edwina's repertoire (see Leverich, p. 567).

Williams' sheer attention to detail in creating this portrait meant that the character of Amanda was at the very heart of the play as originally conceived. After Williams submitted an early treatment to his agent, Audrey Wood, she encouraged him to concentrate his attention on Amanda, and Williams replied that 'yes, the central and most interesting character is certainly Amanda and in the writing the focus would be on her mainly' (quoted Leverich, p. 509). Sure enough, Amanda dominates the stage for large portions of the play, with her chattering monologues and her forceful arguments with her children. And yet she is not, in the final analysis, 'the central character': a play's protagonist needs to be seen to go on an emotional journey and, finally, to be somehow changed by it, but Amanda, of all the characters in *Menagerie*, is the one who changes least. Her final, screaming rage at Tom simply reiterates all the qualities and flaws we have seen throughout the play, as her passionate concern for her daughter's well-being becomes mixed up with selfishness and unthinking cruelty (in a particularly harsh blow, she even refers to Laura as 'a cripple', despite insisting throughout the play that she does not see her as one). Williams, it seems, had to present Amanda as he saw his mother – as an unchangeable force rather than as a dramatic subject capable of emotional evolution. The play is written in such a way that, however much we may come to sympathise with her – understanding that her over-protectiveness, for example, is a result of years of having to hold the family together by sheer force of will – we nevertheless always view Amanda from the outside rather than as a character to identify with directly. We see her, in short, through Tom's eyes.

The challenge for any actor playing Amanda, therefore, is to find her way 'inside' a character that the play itself seems to view from the 'outside' – to inhabit the part in such a way that its external pyrotechnics seem supported by a plausible inner emotional life. For while Amanda is certainly the 'flashiest' part in the play, she is also the hardest for an actor to flesh out convincingly. She is, as one critic observes, 'the play's dominating force. Her asphyxiating, over-protective concern for her grown-up offspring combined with an irritating manner, a genteel dottiness and a tendency to live in the past, requires an actress with a larger than life persona and a formidable technique' (*LTR*, 1995, p. 1279). The play's original production succeeded in large part thanks to the fact that just such a person was found to play Amanda: Laurette Taylor, one of the great stars of the American theatre, who had been out of favour with producers for some years because of her unreliability due to alcoholism, was persuaded to make a final, glorious 'comeback' to play this part. She herself came to see her performance in *Menagerie* as the crowning achievement of her career, and certainly the critics saw that first production as being very much Taylor's show. 'Miss Taylor's perfomance is one of the most superb that I have ever seen in the theatre,' commented the reviewer in New York's *Morning Telegraph*, while the *World Telegram*'s Burton Roscoe noted simply that 'I can't say anything adequate' to describe her: 'You can't describe a sunset. . . . I never hope to see again, in the theatre, anything as perfect.'

In subsequent years, the part of Amanda has been played by a string of star actresses. As one of the few truly complex, challenging roles for middle-aged women in the contemporary repertoire, it has attracted the likes of Helen Hayes (who played Amanda in the London premiere in 1948, and then again in New York in 1956), Maureen Stapleton (who appeared in New York productions in both 1965 and 1975), Jessica Tandy (New York, 1983), Susannah York (London, 1989), Julie Harris (New York, 1994) and Zoë Wanamaker (London, 1995). The part has also been played on screen by Gertrude Lawrence (1950 film version), Katharine Hepburn (1973 television version) and Joanne Woodward (1987 film version). In the hands of such performers, the role of Amanda has been successfully played as the *tour de force* that it is, although Laurette Taylor's performance remains the most celebrated of all.

Today, the part of Amanda is considered the

definitive depiction of the 'ageing Southern belle', a female type who appears in many other plays and movies, always lamenting the loss of the old, pre-Civil War days of debutante balls and gentleman callers. This is so much the case that in 1994, the American playwright Christopher Durang even wrote an affectionate parody of *The Glass Menagerie* entitled *For Whom the Southern Belle Tolls* (in which 'Lawrence' receives a 'feminine caller' who breaks the most treasured swizzle stick in his collection). The portrait of the mother in this play is a satirical pastiche of the stereotypical Southern belle, but one cannot help feeling that Durang has somewhat missed the point of Williams' portrait of Amanda, which is already highly satirical and ironic. Amanda, after all, must have been born in the last decades of the nineteenth century (Edwina was born in 1884), and so is far too young to remember the pre-War days herself (the Civil War lasted from 1861 to 1865). Even assuming that all her romantic memories of her youth are true, they must necessarily be memories of a Southern culture which was, even then, looking backwards to idealised, bygone days. Moreover, Williams makes very clear that Amanda's memories are themselves an inextricable mix of fact and rose-tinted fiction. His decision to portray her attempting to peddle cheap romantic fiction over the telephone is a further, wryly ironic touch: Amanda's picture of herself as a Southern belle seems to owe as much to reading pulp novels like *Gone With the Wind* as it does to her actual youth. Williams, through his portrait of Amanda, cuttingly satirises the tendency of many Southerners of his day to romanticise a golden age that never was. He may also have been thinking of his mother's tendency to 'perform' her own constructed idea of Southernness: the daughter of mid-Westerners from Ohio, Edwina chose to cultivate and maintain a genteel Deep South accent throughout her life, despite living the majority of it in urban St Louis. Clearly, any actor playing Amanda should be careful to explore the emotional complexities lying behind her adoption of stereotypical Southern belle behaviour, rather than simply playing her as a comic old woman. As Williams stresses in his character notes, she must not be played as a type, but as a distinct individual with unique assets and flaws.

Notably, however, one aspect of Amanda's 'Southernness' which Williams does not explore in any detail in the play is her racism. Race issues are dealt with more fully in other Williams works, but in *Menagerie*, Amanda's casual references to 'darkies' and 'niggers' pass without comment. When the play was first written, this would simply have been accepted as a standard (if regrettable) part of the vocabulary of a person like Amanda: for her, blacks are simply the social inferiors she was brought up to regard them as. Yet today – when words such as 'nigger' are particularly inflammatory and controversial – many people are likely to find the play's failure to query Amanda's racism problematic. One option, of course, is simply to cut or change the offending words. In 1989, Washington DC's Arena Stage chose this option when mounting a revival of the play with an all-black cast. Ruby Dee, who played Amanda in that production, rejected criticisms of the casting choice by insisting that the play's story could plausibly apply to a black family as well as a white one, and that even Amanda's memories were believable because there were, in fact, property-owning blacks in the old South. Few reviewers found either the production or Dee's explanation convincing, but it is intriguing to note that two years later, when San Francisco's Lorraine Hansberry Theater also presented an all-black production, the notices were much more favourable. In this instance, not a word of the script had been cut, so a black Amanda was heard to refer to 'the darky'. An unsettling double focus effect was thus created, with the play's language appearing to be contradicted by the visual sign of skin colour: this production did not pretend the Wingfields were a black family, but presented a white family played by black actors. This approach allowed for an implicit critique of Amanda's racism to be apparent in the very staging of the play. It was the kind of overtly theatrical strategy which one suspects Williams himself might have approved of.

Tom

Another controversial issue, which would never have occurred to audiences when the play was first staged, is raised by the unanswered question of exactly where Tom goes at night. He repeatedly insists that he simply goes to the movies, but his story is never entirely convincing, especially as he periodically returns to the apartment in the small hours of the morning, blind drunk. Various critics have suggested in recent years that Tom – like Tennessee Williams himself – might be gay, and that *The Glass Menagerie* can be seen as an example of a 'closet drama' in which homosexuality is never mentioned, but into which those 'in the know' can read a hidden gay subtext. According to this theory, Tom's nocturnal activities might include attending gay bars, which would certainly help explain why he feels unable to discuss his whereabouts with his mother.

There is, however, nothing to support this reading besides speculation, and there are many legitimate objections to it. For one thing, Williams himself did not begin to experiment with homosexuality until after he had left St Louis: during the period of his life fictionalised in *Menagerie*, he was still lusting hopelessly after Hazel Kramer. Accordingly, the character Tom sometimes seems very lonely and unloved – as is most clearly indicated by his reference in Scene Five to his voyeuristic watching of the couples making out in the dark alleyway beside the apartment: 'this was the compensation for lives which passed like mine, without change or adventure' (p. 39). Even so, the debate over where Tom goes at night is indicative of the shadowy uncertainties which seem to shroud this character: despite his being the play's narrator and moving force, he seems to be the one about whose motives and behaviour we can be least sure. It could be argued that Williams, in portraying Tom as a version of his younger self, chose to surround him with ambiguity precisely because he himself felt very uncertain and ambiguous about his own identity at that time. In that sense, the question of Williams' sexual orientation – which was clearly part and parcel of his youthful confusion and anxiety – does perhaps have a significant, subtextual role in the play.

The critic David Savran, who has written very shrewdly on the gay dimensions of Williams' work in his book *Communists, Cowboys and Queers*, could be summing Tom up when he refers to 'the never-quite-whole subject that commandeers Williams's work', who is 'unable to claim the position of "hero" or even "protagonist". Instead, [he] is constantly decentered and dispossessed, stumbling through a dramatic structure that is similarly decentered and unstable' (Savran, p. 98). Whereas Amanda is an intricately drawn, fully filled-out portrait of a woman seen from the outside, Tom is at once a character to whom we have more direct emotional access (as the play's narrator) and of whom we know less. His mysteriousness is underlined, in particular, by the fact that he operates on a hazy borderline between the past events he is describing and the unspecified 'present' from which he narrates to us. In playing the role, an actor must decide whether he is presenting two clearly distinct Toms – older and younger – or whether in fact the older Tom is *reliving* the events himself. The latter possibility would make his behaviour in the scenes themselves even more uncertain (did he 'really' say this 'back then', or is he rewriting his words in retrospect?), and it should be noted that it is this latter possibility that Williams himself seems to call for in specifying that Tom appears at the start 'dressed as a merchant sailor'. Since the actor playing Tom has no opportunity to change into clothes more appropriate to his warehouse-working days (at least during the first scene), we thus see the character enacting the events of his past while wearing the uniform of the future career into which he will escape at the end of the play. Again, it is a shame that this costume specification is a stage direction so often ignored in production, because it underlines vividly the ambiguous doubleness (or even the double vision) which seems to surround Tom throughout the play. The younger Tom needs urgently to leave his family and St Louis, but he also needs to stay, for Laura's sake; the older Tom looks back with fond nostalgia, but also with haunted guilt. As his final speech makes particularly clear, Tom is constantly reliving the past in his present, and the collision of those two worlds seems to be steadily driving him to distraction.

It is interesting to note that Williams himself remained extremely ambivalent about his portrayal of Tom in the play, agreeing with a number of his critics that 'the narrations are not up to the play' (quoted Arnott, p. 23). That judgement is, to the say the least, a questionable one, given that Tom's narrations do so much to contextualise, comment on, and ironise the events depicted in the scenes. The play would be much the poorer (and more sentimental) without the frame of critical perspective which the narrations place around the action. Moreover, without the narrations, we would know still less about Tom, who remains so peripheral to so many of the scenes – watching from the dark like the movie-viewers he describes to Jim in Scene Six, rather than participating directly. The opening of Scene Four, in which Tom comes home drunk at 5 a.m., is one of the few moments in the play when our attention is focused exclusively on Tom's personal conflicts, and even this was a late addition to the text. It was written by Williams to prevent the play's first director Eddie Dowling, who was also playing Tom, from inserting his own drunk scene to give himself a 'star turn' moment. Williams later conceded that the scene he was required to add 'does little harm to the play', but Lyle Leverich is more accurate in his assessment that it is positively beneficial – that Dowling's instincts about what the play needed were right, even if his methods were questionable (see Leverich, pp. 552–3). Williams had written Tom from such a personal, ambivalent perspective that he needed an objective eye to point out where the character needed fleshing out a little. In the final script, Williams strikes just the right balance between mystery and clarity in his characterisation of Tom.

Jim

By comparison with Tom, the role of Jim seems quite straightforward. He is, as Williams specifies in the shortest of his character notes, 'a nice, ordinary young man', and that is indeed, on one level, all that needs to be said about him. Although Tom admits, in his opening narration, to using this character as a symbol more than a person, his comment applies more to the *idea* of the gentleman caller as it is deployed through the first half of the play than it does to Jim himself. In my own 1999 production, we extended our non-naturalistic approach to the play by having the caller visible through most of the first act, as a ghost-like figure standing at the window of the apartment, and occasionally moving through the living space. This idea, which was very effective visually, was inspired by Tom's description of the caller as a 'specter' who 'haunted our small apartment' (p. 19). However, once he was on stage as Jim in Scene Six, the actor playing Jim (Jack Fortescue) found that he had to shed all sense of ghostliness and become very ordinary and human.

Unlike the three Wingfields, Jim is in touch with the realities of the outside world, and seems happy to function according to social conventions such as climbing the career ladder and marrying a nice girl from the same religious background. Indeed he seems, by some distance, to be the most well-adjusted character in the play. He has apparently experienced his fair share of disappointments, which makes him able to sympathise with Laura, and he has dreams and ambitions for himself just as does Tom, but he has managed not to let these haunt him. There is no reason not to suppose that, when he leaves at the end of the play, he will go off to lead a happy, ordinary life with Betty and find a solid (if unspectacular) career in radio or television.

Some have argued that Jim's ordinariness is intended by Williams to be seen as dully oppressive, and certainly the forces of conformity are seen as dangerously destructive in other Williams plays. It might be possible to play Jim as a crass, rather oafish character whose jolly exclamations such as 'comfortable as a cow!' and 'Hey there Mr Light Bulb!' seem grating, and whose dreams of '*Knowledge* – Zzzzp! *Money* – Zzzzzzp! – *Power*!' seem hollow and greedy (p. 82). Yet to do so would be to miss not only the playfulness of these lines ('I guess you think I think a lot of myself!'), but also to remove the emotional depth from Jim's entire encounter with Laura. If he were played as a blundering corporation man, Laura's adoration of him would seem merely foolish, and the aftermath of the kiss between them would lack dramatic tension. An audience has to be convinced that Jim is fundamentally a good person, and to want – for Laura's sake – to see a relationship between the two of them begin to flower. The tragic irony of the situation is only apparent if we are convinced that he is trying to 'do the right thing' – firstly in trying to encourage Laura and bring her out of herself (which leads him, unwittingly, into a romantic entanglement with her), and secondly in deciding to tell her about his fiancée Betty. He himself seems trapped by convention at that point, having to return to his 'steady girl' even though he seems to see something more indefinably radiant in the crippled Laura: both of them thus suffer *because* of his basic decency.

Reviewers of the 1995 London production made a particular point of praising Mark Dexter for his performance as Jim. According to *What's On*'s Graham Hassell, Dexter had 'the personable ebullience of a young James Stewart, a good-intentioned young old fogey' (*LTR*, 1995, p. 1685). The *Financial Times* critic Ian Shuttleworth concurred that 'Jim's smug self-satisfaction [is] offset by a genuine warmth and sympathy', and that Dexter 'is visibly "doing" Jimmy Stewart: there could be no finer model for such a figure' (ibid). In the original 1945 production, Anthony Ross was also singled out by critics – almost as often as Laurette Taylor herself – for his remarkably sympathetic performance as Jim. According to the *Wall Street Journal*, Ross 'did the most perfect job of all'. Interestingly, praise such as this is rarely if ever accorded to actors playing the part of Tom, even though that role might seem, on first inspection, to be the more significant. For where Tom always remains in the margins of the play, a facilitator more than a star player in his own drama, Jim controls the ebb and flow of events in the final, climactic scene between himself and Laura – an encounter described, even as early as 1945, as 'one of the most amazing love scenes ever written' (*New York Journal-American*).

Laura

One of the most notable things about that crucial scene is that Jim and Laura's conversation is somewhat one-sided. Jim, who aspires to social improvement through acquiring skills in public speaking, tends to talk a lot even when he is most nervous (this much he shares with Amanda), whereas Laura rarely speaks in anything other than short, hesitant sentences, and several times retreats into complete silence. The great difficulty for an actor playing Laura, throughout the play, is that the part is primarily *reactive* rather than active: Laura almost always responds to the words and actions of others rather than initiating anything herself. Her responses, moreover, frequently come in the form of loaded silence. Somehow, given very little to work with in terms of dialogue, the actor has to convey an almost unearthly delicacy – to embody the most fragile and vulnerable feelings imaginable by an audience. In this regard, playing Laura is perhaps an even bigger challenge for an actor than playing Amanda.

Tellingly, Williams' intentions for the way Laura is to be perceived are made most apparent not in his character notes (though these are well detailed) but in his lighting suggestions. 'The light upon Laura should be distinct from the others, having a peculiar pristine clarity such as light used in early religious portraits of female saints or madonnas . . . where the figures are radiant in atmosphere that is relatively dusky.' Clearly, while Williams saw Jim as the most bluntly realistic character in the play, Laura – by contrast – is intended to be irridescent, representing the most sheltered and treasured of our inner hopes. How, exactly, is an actor to carry this off? To begin with, there are practical issues to consider, such as not overplaying Laura's limp. If she seems too awkward in her movements (or even grotesquely comic, as I have seen in one misguided instance), the audience may look *at* her with a pity, but will be unlikely to identify *with* her directly. Williams' insistence that Laura's limp 'need not be more than suggested on the stage' is important because it focuses attention not on an actual physical handicap, but on an inner vulnerability: Laura *feels* that her 'clumping' is more obvious than it is because, as Jim astutely observes, she is suffering from an 'inferiority complex' – feeling herself to be worthless in the eyes of the world.

Yet while these considerations can be discussed between director and actor, a successful portayal of Laura is dependent, ultimately, on casting. An actor has to be found who can project a kind of ethereal yet vivid presence, and this is not something which can be learnt or acquired. Notably, in most major productions, casting directors have opted for quite slender actresses – presumably because they can more readily appear fragile. This was certainly true of the original Laura, Julie Haydon, in the 1945 production (Haydon eventually went on to play Amanda in a 1980 New York revival), and more recent Lauras have included waif-like figures such as Amanda Plummer (New York, 1973), Martha Plimpton (Chicago, 1999), and Calista Flockhart – best known as the alarmingly thin star of TV's *Ally McBeal* (New York, 1994). Perhaps the most celebrated performance of Laura to date, however, was that in Sam Mendes's 1995 London production at the Donmar Warehouse: 'Claire Skinner delivers a luminous performance, arousing a magnificent pity without ever becoming simply pitiful,' commented Ian Shuttleworth (*LTR*, 1995, p. 1685). 'The pale, tremulous centre of this production is Claire Skinner's Laura,' concurred *Time Out*'s Jane Edwardes: 'even when her brother and mother are having one of their frequent rows, one's main concern is with what effect it will have on her' (ibid). Such comments suggest that Skinner's award-winning performance was directly in line with Williams' intentions for the part.

Crucially, though, Skinner also demonstrated that the

part requires far more than an emphasis on either physical or mental fragility. Critics were quick to point out the underlying strengths of the character as she played it. Robert Butler, in the *Independent on Sunday*, wrote of Skinner's urgency and freshness, counterbalancing the usual hesitancy and dreaminess, and stressed that, 'above all, she has an exceptional quality of stillness' (*LTR*, 1995, p. 1280). It is important for any production to find such qualities in Laura, so that she does not become merely a victim – and so that the narrative in general does not become merely 'sentimental' or 'mawkish'. This 'tough, delicate masterpiece' of a play (Jeremy Kingston in *The Times*) is made all the more moving because 'the playwright knew, as so many of the subsequent directors have not, to leaven the torment with darts of grim humour; nowhere is this more touching than when Skinner's Laura strives to alleviate Jim's guilt at having accidentally broken the horn off her favourite glass unicorn whilst dancing with her' (Shuttleworth). The moment described here is central to the play, as Laura forces back her desperate disappointment at the damage to her most treasured possession, and tries to assure Jim that 'It doesn't matter. Maybe it's a blessing in disguise' (p. 86). She even jokes about the unicorn being happier now that he can blend in with the other horses and appear 'less freakish', and in so doing she succeeds in putting Jim at ease again despite her own pain. This is a key example of the hidden emotional strength which Laura demonstrates at pivotal moments throughout the play (another one comes minutes later as she gives Jim the unicorn as 'a souvenir'). In performances such as Claire Skinner's, one realises that Laura is, paradoxically, the most resilient of the characters in the play, as well as the most delicate.

And yet if this is the case, we must ask whether Tom's despairing guilt at the end of the play is justified or not. The closing narrative suggests that, in leaving St Louis, Tom has abandoned Laura to some terrible fate of loneliness and isolation, yet Tom can be wrong – as the play makes very clear. Desperate regret may indeed have been Williams' legitimate feelings about his own sister's committal to a mental institution, but there is nothing in the play besides Tom's narrative to suggest that Laura has been consigned to a similarly hopeless fate. Indeed, if anything, the unexpected strength she finds with which to comfort Jim for his blundering suggests that she might be able to find it in herself to recover from the blows she receives. Perhaps the damage Jim causes really is 'a blessing in disguise'. In my own 1999 production, Elly Reid – playing Laura – found that one of the most crucial moments in deciding her character's fate was the 'Yes!' which Laura utters after Amanda asks her whether or not she wishes the best for Jim in the future (p. 94). This is also Laura's final line in the play, and if it is delivered in a downbeat or tearful way, Laura is left appearing broken and empty. Yet if, as Elly chose to do, Laura looks up with a smile, fighting back her own sadness in order to bless Jim, to thank him for his goodness to her, then a quite different possibility is registered. Perhaps, we speculate, she can now find it in herself to 'get over' Jim, and move on. In our production, at the moment in Tom's final speech when he speaks of feeling his sister touch his shoulder, Laura actually did step up to him, place a hand on his shoulder, and look longingly at him as if to say – across time and space – 'Tom, please don't torture yourself, I'm doing fine!' Tom, of course, remained lost in his own torments, but many audience members commented how unexpectedly hopeful they found the play's ending, as a result of the way Elly played it.

Our approach to the play was partially inspired by Paula Killen's one-woman show, *Still Life with Blue Roses* (Chicago, 1997) – one of a growing number of creative responses to *The Glass Menagerie* (others include Durang's *For Whom the Southern Belle Tolls* and a 1993 dance adaptation by New York's Classic Stage Company, intriguingly entitled *Faith Healing*). Killen, clearly a great admirer of the play, took as her starting point the fact that Laura, although central to *Menagerie*, never really has the chance to speak for herself. In the first part of *Still Life with Blue Roses*, she sits on a couch in a candlelit set reminiscent of that in *Menagerie*, and – as Laura – explains to the audience that, while she appreciates Tom's efforts to write about her, she wishes that he had made the effort to find out how she really felt about things. Killen's wryly amusing commentary is, implicitly, a feminist critique of the tendency of male authors to place their female characters in silenced positions where they seem powerless to help themselves, and are dependent on or subjected to the actions of men (in this case, Jim and Tom, who both leave Laura abandoned). Turning this situation on its head, Killen has her Laura leave St Louis. Part two of *Still Life* is in the form of a public lecture, as Laura presents a sequence of film clips to her audience, documenting her attempts to move to Hollywood and make a movie of her life. Again the presentation is both very funny (especially her attempts to get the casting right) and very poignant, making full use of imagery and titles from Williams' neglected ideas for projections to form a new narrative in which Laura takes control of her life as a modern, media-conscious woman. The irony is – probably quite deliberately on Killen's part – that one is left by the end with a real sense of loss, a feeling that Laura's fragile uniqueness has somehow been mislaid amid the rough and tumble of modern life, and that she (like her unicorn before her) has become 'just like all the others'.

Responding to *Still Life with Blue Roses*, I wanted to see if it was possible to present *Menagerie* in such a way as to bring out a sense that Laura, though largely silent, is still in some way the author of her own narrative, rather than the helpless puppet of Tom's. We discovered, interestingly, that there are numerous points in the play which lend themselves to this idea. Even moments as simple as when she accidentally calls Jim 'Freckles' can be rendered in such a way as to suggest that such a slip betrays a whole world of private passions which remain hidden within her, but which might one day begin to find their way out into the world. Still more telling, in our production, was the point in Scene Four when Tom falls asleep, as Laura watches over him. At this point, a simple glance from Laura up to the audience was enough to suggest that, just maybe, she is quietly presenting us with a kind of alternative narrative to Tom's own story. He believes himself to be in control of the memories he is presenting, but in moments such as those when he 'sleeps' or is absent from the stage, we can perhaps glimpse another possibility.

Experiments such as this one demonstrate clearly that there are many different ways to approach *The Glass Menagerie*, and many possible readings to be found. Far from being the mawkishly sentimental piece it is sometimes thought to be by those who have not properly explored its many layers of emotion, wit, irony and theatrical inventiveness, *Menagerie* remains a rich source of material to be tapped afresh by each new generation of actors, directors and designers. Yet while it is demonstrably a play which constantly lends itself to new interpretations and adaptations, it also remains, at base, a very simple and moving narrative about a family, which has the power to speak to us all about memory and loss, love and hope.

Further Reading

Arnott, Catherine M. (ed.). 1985. *File on Tennessee Williams*, London: Methuen

Bigsby, C.W.E. 1984. *A Critical Introduction to Twentieth-Century American Drama: Volume Two: Williams/Miller/Albee*, Cambridge: Cambridge University Press

Bigsby, Christopher. 1992. *Modern American Drama, 1945–1990.* Cambridge: Cambridge University Press

1997. 'Entering *The Glass Menagerie*', in Matthew C. Roudané (ed.), *The Cambridge Companion to Tennessee Williams* (see below)

Bloom, Harold (ed.). 1988. *The Glass Menagerie: Modern Critical Interpretations*, New York: Chelsea House

Devlin, Albert (ed.). 1986. *Conversations with Tennessee Williams*, Jackson: University Press of Mississippi

Kolin, Philip C. (ed.), 2004. *The Tennessee Williams Encyclopedia*, Westport, CT, and London: Greenwood Press.

Leverich, Lyle. 1995. *Tom: The Unknown Tennessee Williams*, London: Sceptre

Murphy, Brenda. 1992. *Tennessee Williams and Elia Kazan: A Collaboration in the Theatre*, Cambridge: Cambridge University Press

Paller Michael, 2005. *Gentleman Callers: Tennessee Williams, Homosexuality, and Mid-Twentieth-Century Drama*, London and New York: Palgrave Macmillan.

Robinson, Marc. 1994. *The Other American Drama*, Cambridge: Cambridge University Press

Roudané, Matthew C. (ed.). 1997. *The Cambridge Companion to Tennessee Williams*, Cambridge: Cambridge University Press

Savran, David. 1992. *Communists, Cowboys and Queers: The Politics of Masculinity in the Work of Arthur Miller and Tennessee Williams*, Minneapolis: University of Minnesota Press

Spoto, Donald. 1985. *The Kindness of Strangers: The Life of Tennessee Williams*, Boston: Little Brown

Windham, Donald (ed.). 1996. *Tennessee Williams' Letters to Donald Windham, 1940–1965*, London: Brown Thrasher

Williams, Dakin and Shepherd Mead. 1983. *Tennessee Williams: An Intimate Biography*, New York: Arbor House

Williams, Edwina Dakin, as told to Lucy Freeman. 1963. *Remember Me to Tom*, New York: Putnam

Williams, Tennessee. 1945. *Twenty-Seven Wagons Full of Cotton and Other Plays*, New York: New Directions

1948. *American Blues: Five Short Plays*, New York: Dramatists Play Service

1952. *The Roman Spring of Mrs Stone* (novel), London: Lehmann

1957. *One Arm and Other Stories* (revised ed.), New York: New Directions

1958. *The Rose Tattoo* and *Camino Real*, Harmondsworth: Penguin

1962. *A Streetcar Named Desire, The Glass Menagerie* and *Sweet Bird of Youth*, Harmondsworth: Penguin

1968. *Baby Doll, Suddenly Last Summer* and *Something Unspoken*, Harmondsworth: Penguin

1970. *Dragon Country: A Book of Plays*, New York: New Directions
1976. *Cat on a Hot Tin Roof, The Milk Train Doesn't Stop Here Anymore* and *Night of the Iguana*, Harmondsworth: Penguin
1971–1992. *The Theatre of Tennessee Williams*, eight volumes, New York: New Directions
1984. *A Streetcar Named Desire* (student edition), London: Methuen Drama
1989. *Period of Adjustment, Summer and Smoke* and *Small Craft Warnings*, Harmondsworth: Penguin
1996. *Something Cloudy, Something Clear*, London: Methuen Drama
1998. *Not About Nightingales*, London: Methuen Drama

The Glass Menagerie

Nobody, not even the rain, has such small hands.
e. e. cummings

CAST LISTING

The Glass Menagerie was first produced by Eddie Dowling and Louis J. Singer at the Civic Theatre, Chicago, Illinois, on December 26, 1944, and at the Playhouse Theatre, New York City, on March 31, 1945. The setting was designed and lighted by Jo Mielziner; original music was composed by Paul Bowles; the play was staged by Eddie Dowling and Margo Jones. The cast was as follows:

THE MOTHER	LAURETTE TAYLOR
HER SON	EDDIE DOWLING
HER DAUGHTER	JULIE HAYDON
THE GENTLEMAN CALLER	ANTHONY ROSS

SCENE

SCENE: *An alley in St. Louis*

Part I. Preparation for a Gentleman Caller.
Part II. The Gentleman calls.

TIME: *Now and the Past*

THE CHARACTERS

AMANDA WINGFIELD *(the mother)*

A little woman of great but confused vitality clinging frantically to another time and place. Her characterization must be carefully created, not copied from type. She is not paranoiac, but her life is paranoia. There is much to admire in Amanda, and as much to love and pity as there is to laugh at. Certainly she has endurance and a kind of heroism, and though her foolishness makes her unwittingly cruel at times, there is tenderness in her slight person.

LAURA WINGFIELD *(her daughter)*

Amanda, having failed to establish contact with reality, continues to live vitally in her illusions, but Laura's situation is even graver. A childhood illness has left her crippled, one leg slightly shorter than the other, and held in a brace.This defect need not be more than suggested on the stage. Stemming from this, Laura's separation increases till she is like a piece of her own glass collection, too exquisitely fragile to move from the shelf.

TOM WINGFIELD *(her son)*

And the narrator of the play. A poet with a job in a warehouse. His nature is not remorseless, but to escape from a trap he has to act without pity.

JIM O'CONNOR *(the gentleman caller)*

A nice, ordinary, young man.

PRODUCTION NOTES

Being a "memory play," *The Glass Menagerie* can be presented with unusual freedom of convention. Because of its considerably delicate or tenuous material, atmospheric touches and subtleties of direction play a particularly important part. Expressionism and all other unconventional techniques in drama have only one valid aim, and that is a closer approach to truth. When a play employs unconventional techniques, it is not, or certainly shouldn't be, trying to escape its responsibility of dealing with reality, or interpreting experience, but is actually or should be attempting to find a closer approach, a more penetrating and vivid expression of things as they are. The straight realistic play with its genuine Frigidaire and authentic ice-cubes, its characters who speak exactly as its audience speaks, corresponds to the academic landscape and has the same virtue of a photographic likeness. Everyone should know nowadays the unimportance of the photographic in art: that truth, life, or reality is an organic thing which the poetic imagination can represent or suggest, in essence, only through transformation, through changing into other forms than those which were merely present in appearance.

These remarks are not meant as a preface only to this particular play. They have to do with a conception of a new, plastic theatre which must take the place of the exhausted theatre of realistic conventions if the theatre is to resume vitality as a part of our culture.

THE SCREEN DEVICE: There is *only one important difference between the original and the acting version of the play* and that is the *omission* in the latter of the device that I tentatively included in my *original* script. This device was the use of a screen on which were projected magic-lantern slides bearing images or titles. I do not regret the omission of this device from the original Broadway production. The extraordinary power of Miss Taylor's performance made it suitable to have the utmost simplicity in the physical production. But I think it may be interesting to some readers to see how this device was conceived. So I am putting it into the published manuscript. These images and legends, projected from behind, were cast on a section of wall between the front-room and dining-room areas, which should be indistinguishable from the rest when not in use.

The purpose of this will probably be apparent. It is to give accent to certain values in each scene. Each scene contains a particular point (or several) which is structurally the most important. In an episodic play, such as this, the basic structure or narrative line may be obscured from the audience; the effect may seem fragmentary rather than architectural. This may not be the fault of the play so much as a lack of attention in the audience. The legend or image upon the screen will strengthen the effect of what is merely allusion in the writing and allow the primary point to be made more simply and lightly than if the entire responsibility were on the spoken lines. Aside from this structural value, I think the screen will have a definite emotional appeal, less definable but just as important. An imaginative producer or director may invent many other uses for this device than those indicated in the present script. In fact the possibilities of the device seem much larger to me than the instance of this play can possibly utilize.

THE MUSIC: Another extra-literary accent in this play is provided by the use of music. A single recurring tune, "The Glass Menagerie," is used to give emotional emphasis to suitable passages. This tune is like circus music, not when you are on the grounds or in the immediate vicinity of the parade, but when you are at some distance and very likely thinking of something else. It seems under those circumstances to continue almost interminably and it weaves in and out of your preoccupied consciousness; then it is the lightest, most delicate music in the world and perhaps the saddest. It expresses the surface vivacity of life with the underlying strain of immutable and inexpressible sorrow. When you look at a piece of delicately spun glass you think of two things: how beautiful it is and how easily it can be broken. Both of those ideas should be woven into the recurring tune, which dips in and out of the play as if it were carried on a wind that changes. It serves as a thread of connection and allusion between the narrator with his separate point in time and space and the subject of his story. Between each episode it returns as reference to the emotion, nostalgia, which is the first condition of the play. It is primarily Laura's music and therefore comes out most clearly when the play focuses upon her and the lovely fragility of glass which is her image.

THE LIGHTING: The lighting in the play is not realistic. In keeping with the atmosphere of memory, the stage is dim. Shafts of light are focused on selected areas or actors, sometimes in contradistinction to what is the apparent center. For instance, in the quarrel scene between Tom and Amanda, in which Laura has no active part, the clearest pool of light is on her figure. This is also true of the supper scene, when her silent figure on the sofa should remain the visual center. The light upon Laura should be distinct from the others, having a peculiar pristine clarity such as light used in early religious portraits of female saints or madonnas. A certain correspondence to light in religious paintings, such as El Greco's, where the figures are radiant in atmosphere that is relatively dusky, could be effectively used throughout the play. (It will also permit a more effective use of the screen.) A free, imaginative use of light can be of enormous value in giving a mobile, plastic quality to plays of a more or less static nature.

Tennessee Williams

SCENE ONE

The Wingfield apartment is in the rear of the building, one of those vast hive-like conglomerations of cellular living-units that flower as warty growths in overcrowded urban centers of lower middle-class population and are symptomatic of the impulse of this largest and fundamentally enslaved section of American society to avoid fluidity and differentiation and to exist and function as one interfused mass of automatism.

The apartment faces an alley and is entered by a fire escape, a structure whose name is a touch of accidental poetic truth, for all of these huge buildings are always burning with the slow and implacable fires of human desperation. The fire escape is part of what we see—that is, the landing of it and steps descending from it.

The scene is memory and is therefore nonrealistic. Memory takes a lot of poetic license. It omits some details; others are exaggerated, according to the emotional value of the articles it touches, for memory is seated predominantly in the heart. The interior is therefore rather dim and poetic.

At the rise of the curtain, the audience is faced with the dark, grim rear wall of the Wingfield tenement. This building is flanked on both sides by dark, narrow alleys which run into murky canyons of tangled clotheslines, garbage cans, and the sinister latticework of neighboring fire escapes. It is up and down these side alleys that exterior entrances and exits are made during the play. At the end of Tom's opening commentary, the dark tenement wall slowly becomes transparent and reveals the interior of the ground-floor Wingfield apartment.

Nearest the audience is the living room, which also serves as a sleeping room for Laura, the sofa unfolding to make her bed. Just beyond, separated from the living room by a wide arch or second proscenium with transparent faded portieres (or second curtain), is the dining room. In an old-fashioned whatnot in the living room are seen scores of transparent glass animals. A blown-up photograph of the father hangs on the wall of the living room, to the left of the archway. It is the face of a very handsome young man in a doughboy's First World War cap. He is gallantly smiling, ineluctably smiling, as if to say "I will be smiling forever."

Also hanging on the wall, near the photograph, are a typewriter keyboard chart and a Gregg shorthand diagram. An upright typewriter on a small table stands beneath the charts.

The audience hears and sees the opening scene in the dining room through both the transparent fourth wall of the building and the transparent gauze portieres of the dining-room arch. It is during this revealing scene that the fourth wall slowly ascends, out of sight. This transparent exterior wall is not brought down again until the very end of the play, during Tom's final speech.

The narrator is an undisguised convention of the play. He takes whatever license with dramatic convention is convenient to his purposes.

Tom enters, dressed as a merchant sailor, and strolls across to the fire escape. There he stops and lights a cigarette. He addresses the audience.

TOM: Yes, I have tricks in my pocket, I have things up my sleeve. But I am the opposite of a stage magician. He gives you illusion that has the appearance of truth. I give you truth in the pleasant disguise of illusion.

To begin with, I turn back time. I reverse it to that quaint period, the thirties, when the huge middle class of America was matriculating in a school for the blind. Their eyes had failed them, or they had failed their eyes, and so they were having their fingers pressed forcibly down on the fiery Braille alphabet of a dissolving economy.

In Spain there was revolution. Here there was only shouting and confusion. In Spain there was Guernica. Here there were disturbances of labor, sometimes pretty violent, in otherwise peaceful cities such as Chicago, Cleveland, Saint Louis . . . This is the social background of the play.

[*Music begins to play.*]

The play is memory. Being a memory play, it is dimly lighted, it is sentimental, it is not realistic. In memory everything seems to happen to music. That explains the fiddle in the wings.

I am the narrator of the play, and also a character in it. The other characters are my mother, Amanda, my sister, Laura, and a gentleman caller who appears in the final scenes. He is the most realistic character in the play, being an emissary from a world of reality that we were somehow set apart from. But since I have a poet's weakness for symbols, I am using this character also as a symbol; he is the long-delayed but always expected something that we live for.

There is a fifth character in the play who doesn't appear except in this larger-than-life-size photograph over the mantel. This is our father who left us a long time ago. He was a telephone man who fell in love with long distances; he gave up his job with the telephone company and skipped the light fantastic out of town . . .

The last we heard of him was a picture postcard from Mazatlan, on the Pacific coast of Mexico, containing a message of two words: "Hello—Goodbye!" and no address.

I think the rest of the play will explain itself. . . .

[*Amanda's voice becomes audible through the portieres.*]

[*Legend on screen:* "Ou sont les neiges."]

[*Tom divides the portieres and enters the dining room. Amanda and Laura are seated at a drop-leaf table. Eating is indicated by gestures without food or utensils. Amanda faces the audience. Tom and Laura are seated in profile. The interior has lit up softly and through the scrim we see Amanda and Laura seated at the table.*]

AMANDA [*calling*]: Tom?

TOM: Yes, Mother.

AMANDA: We can't say grace until you come to the table!

TOM: Coming, Mother. [*He bows slightly and withdraws, reappearing a few moments later in his place at the table.*]

AMANDA [*to her son*]: Honey, don't *push* with your *fingers.* If you have to push with something, the thing to push with is a crust of bread. And chew—chew! Animals have secretions in their stomachs which enable them to digest food without mastication, but human beings are supposed to chew their food before they swallow it down. Eat food leisurely, son, and really enjoy it. A well-cooked meal has lots of delicate flavors that have to be held in the mouth for appreciation. So chew your food and give your salivary glands a chance to function!

[*Tom deliberately lays his imaginary fork down and pushes his chair back from the table.*]

TOM: I haven't enjoyed one bite of this dinner because of your constant directions on how to eat it. It's you that make me rush through meals with your hawklike attention to every bite I take. Sickening—spoils my appetite—all this discussion of—animals' secretion—salivary glands—mastication!

AMANDA [*lightly*]: Temperament like a Metropolitan star!

[*Tom rises and walks toward the living room.*]

You're not excused from the table.

TOM: I'm getting a cigarette.

AMANDA: You smoke too much.

[*Laura rises.*]

LAURA: I'll bring in the blanc mange.

[*Tom remains standing with his cigarette by the portieres.*]

AMANDA [*rising*]: No, sister, no, sister—you be the lady this time and I'll be the darky.

LAURA: I'm already up.

AMANDA: Resume your seat, little sister—I want you to stay fresh and pretty—for gentlemen callers!

LAURA [*sitting down*]: I'm not expecting any gentlemen callers.

AMANDA [*crossing out to the kitchenette, airily*]: Sometimes they come when they are least expected! Why, I remember one Sunday afternoon in Blue Mountain—

[*She enters the kitchenette.*]

TOM: I know what's coming!

LAURA: Yes. But let her tell it.

TOM: Again?

LAURA: She loves to tell it.

[*Amanda returns with a bowl of dessert*].

AMANDA: One Sunday afternoon in Blue Mountain—your mother received—*seventeen!*—gentlemen callers! Why, sometimes there weren't chairs enough to accommodate them all. We had to send the nigger over to bring in folding chairs from the parish house.

TOM [*remaining at the portieres*]: How did you entertain those gentlemen callers?

AMANDA: I understood the art of conversation!

TOM: I bet you could talk.

AMANDA: Girls in those days *knew* how to talk, I can tell you.

TOM: Yes?

[*Image on screen*: Amanda as a girl on a porch, greeting callers.]

AMANDA: They knew how to entertain their gentlemen callers. It wasn't enough for a girl to be possessed of a pretty face and a graceful figure—although I wasn't slighted in either respect. She also needed to have a nimble wit and a tongue to meet all occasions.

TOM: What did you talk about?

AMANDA: Things of importance going on in the world! Never anything coarse or common or vulgar.

[*She addresses Tom as though he were seated in the vacant chair at the table though he remains by the portieres. He plays this scene as though reading from a script.*]

My callers were gentlemen—all! Among my callers were some of the most prominent young planters of the Mississippi Delta—planters and sons of planters!

[*Tom motions for music and a spot of light on Amanda. Her eyes lift, her face glows, her voice becomes rich and elegiac.*]

[*Screen legend*: "Ou sont les neiges d'antan?"]

There was young Champ Laughlin who later became vice-president of the Delta Planters Bank. Hadley Stevenson who was drowned in Moon Lake and left his widow one hundred and fifty thousand in Government bonds. There were the Cutrere brothers, Wesley and Bates. Bates was one of my bright particular beaux! He got in a quarrel with that wild Wainwright boy. They shot it out on the floor of Moon Lake Casino. Bates was shot through the stomach. Died in the ambulance on his way to Memphis. His widow was also well provided-for, came into eight or ten thousand acres, that's all. She married him on the rebound—never loved her—carried my picture on him the night he died! And there was that boy that every girl in the Delta had set her cap for! That beautiful, brilliant young Fitzhugh boy from Greene County!

TOM: What did he leave his widow?

AMANDA: He never married! Gracious, you talk as though all of my old admirers had turned up their toes to the daisies!

TOM: Isn't this the first you've mentioned that still survives?

AMANDA: That Fitzhugh boy went North and made a fortune—came to be known as the Wolf of Wall Street! He had the Midas touch, whatever he touched turned to gold! And I could have been Mrs. Duncan J. Fitzhugh, mind you! But—I picked your *father!*

LAURA [*rising*]: Mother, let me clear the table.

AMANDA: No, dear, you go in front and study your typewriter chart. Or practice your shorthand a little. Stay fresh and pretty!—It's almost time for our gentlemen callers to start arriving. [*She flounces girlishly toward the kitchenette*] How many do you suppose we're going to entertain this afternoon?

[*Tom throws down the paper and jumps up with a groan.*]

LAURA [*alone in the dining room*]: I don't believe we're going to receive any, Mother.

AMANDA [*reappearing, airily*]: What? No one—not one? You must be joking!

[*Laura nervously echoes her laugh. She slips in a fugitive manner through the half-open portieres and draws them gently behind her. A shaft of very clear light is thrown on her face against the faded tapestry of the curtains. Faintly the music of "The Glass Menagerie" is heard as she continues, lightly*:]

Not one gentleman caller? It can't be true! There must be a flood, there must have been a tornado!

LAURA: It isn't a flood, it's not a tornado, Mother. I'm just not popular like you were in Blue Mountain. . . .

[*Tom utters another groan. Laura glances at him with a faint, apologetic smile. Her voice catches a little*:]

Mother's afraid I'm going to be an old maid.

[*The scene dims out with the "Glass Menagerie" music.*]

SCENE TWO

On the dark stage the screen is lighted with the image of blue roses. Gradually Laura's figure becomes apparent and the screen goes out. The music subsides.

Laura is seated in the delicate ivory chair at the small claw-foot table. She wears a dress of soft violet material for a kimono—her hair is tied back from her forehead with a ribbon. She is washing and polishing her collection of glass. Amanda appears on the fire escape steps. At the sound of her ascent, Laura catches her breath, thrusts the bowl of ornaments away, and seats herself stiffly before the diagram of the typewriter keyboard as though it held her spellbound. Something has happened to Amanda. It is written in her face as she climbs to the landing: a look that is grim and hopeless and a little absurd. She has on one of those cheap or imitation velvety-looking cloth coats with imitation fur collar. Her hat is five or six years old, one of those dreadful cloche hats that were worn in the late Twenties, and she is clutching an enormous black patent-leather pocketbook with nickel clasps and initials. This is her full-dress outfit, the one she usually wears to the D.A.R. Before entering she looks through the door. She purses her lips, opens her eyes very wide, rolls them upward and shakes her head. Then she slowly lets herself in the door. Seeing her mother's expression Laura touches her lips with a nervous gesture.

LAURA: Hello, Mother, I was— [*She makes a nervous gesture toward the chart on the wall. Amanda leans against the shut door and stares at Laura with a martyred look.*]

AMANDA: Deception? Deception? [*She slowly removes her hat and gloves, continuing the sweet suffering stare. She lets the hat and gloves fall on the floor—a bit of acting.*]

LAURA [*shakily*]: How was the D.A.R. meeting?

[*Amanda slowly opens her purse and removes a dainty white handkerchief which she shakes out delicately and delicately touches to her lips and nostrils.*]

Didn't you go to the D.A.R. meeting, Mother?

AMANDA [*faintly, almost inaudibly*]: —No.—No. [*then more forcibly:*] I did not have the strength—to go to the D.A.R. In fact, I did not have the courage! I wanted to find a hole in the ground and hide myself in it forever! [*She crosses slowly to the wall and removes the diagram of the typewriter keyboard. She holds it in front of her for a second, staring at it sweetly and sorrowfully—then bites her lips and tears it in two pieces.*]

LAURA [*faintly*]: Why did you do that, Mother?

[*Amanda repeats the same procedure with the chart of the Gregg Alphabet.*]

Why are you—

AMANDA: Why? Why? How old are you, Laura?

LAURA: Mother, you know my age.

AMANDA: I thought that you were an adult; it seems that I was mistaken. [*She crosses slowly to the sofa and sinks down and stares at Laura.*]

LAURA: Please don't stare at me, Mother.

[*Amanda closes her eyes and lowers her head. There is a ten-second pause.*]

AMANDA: What are we going to do, what is going to become of us, what is the future?

[*There is another pause.*]

LAURA: Has something happened, Mother?

[*Amanda draws a long breath, takes out the handkerchief again, goes through the dabbing process.*]

Mother, has—something happened?

AMANDA: I'll be all right in a minute, I'm just bewildered —[*She hesitates.*]—by life. . . .

LAURA: Mother, I wish that you would tell me what's happened!

AMANDA: As you know, I was supposed to be inducted into my office at the D.A.R. this afternoon.

[*Screen image*: A swarm of typewriters.]

But I stopped off at Rubicam's Business College to speak to your teachers about your having a cold and ask them what progress they thought you were making down there.

LAURA: Oh. . . .

AMANDA: I went to the typing instructor and introduced myself as your mother. She didn't know who you were. "Wingfield," she said, "We don't have any such student enrolled at the school!"
I assured her she did, that you had been going to classes since early in January.
"I wonder," she said, "If you could be talking about that terribly shy little girl who dropped out of school after only a few days' attendance?"
"No," I said, "Laura, my daughter, has been going to school every day for the past six weeks!"
"Excuse me," she said. She took the attendance book out and there was your name, unmistakably printed, and all the dates you were absent until they decided that you had dropped out of school.

I still said, "No, there must have been some mistake! There must have been some mix-up in the records!"
And she said, "No—I remember her perfectly now. Her hands shook so that she couldn't hit the right keys! The first time we gave a speed test, she broke down completely—was sick at the stomach and almost had to be carried into the wash room! After that morning she never showed up any more. We phoned the house but never got any answer"—While I was working at Famous–Barr, I suppose, demonstrating those—

[*She indicates a brassiere with her hands.*]

Oh! I felt so weak I could barely keep on my feet! I had to sit down while they got me a glass of water! Fifty dollars' tuition, all of our plans—my hopes and ambitions for you—just gone up the spout, just gone up the spout like that.

[*Laura draws a long breath and gets awkwardly to her feet. She crosses to the Victrola and winds it up.*]

What are you doing?

LAURA: Oh! [*She releases the handle and returns to her seat.*]

AMANDA: Laura, where have you been going when you've gone out pretending that you were going to business college?

LAURA: I've just been going out walking.

AMANDA: That's not true.

LAURA: It is. I just went walking.

AMANDA: Walking? Walking? In winter? Deliberately courting pneumonia in that light coat? Where did you walk to, Laura?

LAURA: All sorts of places—mostly in the park.

AMANDA: Even after you'd started catching that cold?

LAURA: It was the lesser of two evils, Mother.

[*Screen image*: Winter scene in a park.]

I couldn't go back there. I—threw up—on the floor!

AMANDA: From half past seven till after five every day you mean to tell me you walked around in the park, because you wanted to make me think that you were still going to Rubicam's Business College?

LAURA: It wasn't as bad as it sounds. I went inside places to get warmed up.

AMANDA: Inside where?

LAURA: I went in the art museum and the bird houses at the Zoo. I visited the penguins every day! Sometimes I did without lunch and went to the movies. Lately I've been spending most of my afternoons in the Jewel Box, that big glass house where they raise the tropical flowers.

AMANDA: You did all this to deceive me, just for deception?

[*Laura looks down.*] Why?

LAURA: Mother, when you're disappointed, you get that awful suffering look on your face, like the picture of Jesus' mother in the museum!

AMANDA: Hush!

LAURA: I couldn't face it.

[*There is a pause. A whisper of strings is heard. Legend on screen*: "The Crust of Humility."]

AMANDA [*hopelessly fingering the huge pocketbook*]: So what are we going to do the rest of our lives? Stay home and

watch the parades go by? Amuse ourselves with the glass menagerie, darling? Eternally play those worn-out phonograph records your father left as a painful reminder of him? We won't have a business career—we've given that up because it gave us nervous indigestion! [*She laughs wearily.*] What is there left but dependency all our lives? I know so well what becomes of unmarried women who aren't prepared to occupy a position. I've seen such pitiful cases in the South—barely tolerated spinsters living upon the grudging patronage of sister's husband or brother's wife!—stuck away in some little mousetrap of a room—encouraged by one in-law to visit another—little birdlike women without any nest—eating the crust of humility all their life!
Is that the future that we've mapped out for ourselves? I swear it's the only alternative I can think of! [*She pauses.*] It isn't a very pleasant alternative, is it? [*She pauses again.*] Of course—some girls *do marry.*

[*Laura twists her hands nervously.*]

Haven't you ever liked some boy?

LAURA: Yes. I liked one once. [*She rises.*] I came across his picture a while ago.

AMANDA [*with some interest*]: He gave you his picture?

LAURA: No, it's in the yearbook.

AMANDA [*disappointed*]: Oh—a high school boy.

[*Screen image*: Jim as the high school hero bearing a silver cup.]

LAURA: Yes. His name was Jim. [*She lifts the heavy annual from the claw-foot table.*] Here he is in *The Pirates of Penzance.*

AMANDA [*absently*]: The what?

LAURA: The operetta the senior class put on. He had a wonderful voice and we sat across the aisle from each other Mondays, Wednesdays and Fridays in the Aud. Here he is with the silver cup for debating! See his grin?

AMANDA [*absently*]: He must have had a jolly disposition.

LAURA: He used to call me—Blue Roses.

[*Screen image*: Blue roses.]

AMANDA: Why did he call you such a name as that?

LAURA: When I had that attack of pleurosis—he asked me what was the matter when I came back. I said pleurosis—he thought that I said Blue Roses! So that's what he always called me after that. Whenever he saw me, he'd holler, "Hello, Blue Roses!" I didn't care for the girl that he went out with. Emily Meisenbach. Emily was the best-dressed girl at Soldan. She never struck me, though, as being sincere . . . It says in the Personal Section—they're engaged. That's—six years ago! They must be married by now.

AMANDA: Girls that aren't cut out for business careers usually wind up married to some nice man. [*She gets up with a spark of revival.*] Sister, that's what you'll do!

[*Laura utters a startled, doubtful laugh. She reaches quickly for a piece of glass.*]

LAURA: But, Mother—

AMANDA: Yes? [*She goes over to the photograph.*]

LAURA [*in a tone of frightened apology*]: I'm—crippled!

AMANDA: Nonsense! Laura, I've told you never, never to use that word. Why, you're not crippled, you just have a little defect—hardly noticeable, even! When people have some slight disadvantage like that, they cultivate other things to make up for it—develop charm—and vivacity—and—*charm!* That's all you have to do! [*She turns again to the photograph.*] One thing your father had *plenty of*—was *charm!*

[*The scene fades out with music.*]

SCENE THREE

Legend on screen: "After the fiasco—"

Tom speaks from the fire escape landing.

TOM: After the fiasco at Rubicam's Business College, the idea of getting a gentleman caller for Laura began to play a more and more important part in Mother's calculations. It became an obsession. Like some archetype of the universal unconscious, the image of the gentleman caller haunted our small apartment. . . .

[*Screen image*: A young man at the door of a house with flowers.]

An evening at home rarely passed without some allusion to this image, this specter, this hope. . . . Even when he wasn't mentioned, his presence hung in Mother's preoccupied look and in my sister's frightened, apologetic manner—hung like a sentence passed upon the Wingfields!
Mother was a woman of action as well as words. She began to take logical steps in the planned direction. Late that winter and in the early spring—realizing that extra money would be needed to properly feather the nest and plume the bird—she conducted a vigorous campaign on the telephone, roping in subscribers to one of those magazines for matrons called *The Homemaker's Companion,* the type of journal that features the serialized sublimations of ladies of letters who think in terms of delicate cuplike breasts, slim, tapering waists, rich, creamy thighs, eyes like wood smoke in autumn, fingers that soothe and caress like strains of music, bodies as powerful as Etruscan sculpture.

[*Screen image*: The cover of a glamor magazine.]

[*Amanda enters with the telephone on a long extension cord. She is spotlighted in the dim stage.*]

AMANDA: Ida Scott? This is Amanda Wingfield! We *missed* you at the D.A.R. last Monday! I said to myself: She's probably suffering with that sinus condition! How is that sinus condition?
Horrors! Heaven have mercy!—You're a Christian martyr, yes, that's what your are, a Christian martyr!
Well, I just now happened to notice that your subscription to the *Companion*'s about to expire! Yes, it expires with the next issue, honey!—just when that wonderful new serial by Bessie Mae Hopper is getting off to such an exciting start. Oh, honey, it's something that you can't miss! You remember how *Gone with the Wind* took everybody by storm? You simply couldn't go out if you hadn't read it. All everybody *talked* was Scarlett O'Hara. Well, this is a book that critics already compare to *Gone with the Wind*. It's the *Gone with the Wind* of the post-World-War generation!—What?—Burning?—Oh, honey, don't let them burn, go take a look in the oven and I'll hold the wire! Heavens—I think she's hung up!

[*The scene dims out.*]

[*Legend on screen*: "You think I'm in love with Continental Shoemakers?"]

[*Before the lights come up again, the violent voices of Tom and Amanda are heard. They are quarreling behind the portieres. In front of them stands Laura with clenched hands and panicky expression. A clear pool of light is on her figure throughout this scene.*]

TOM: What in Christ's name am I—

AMANDA [*shrilly*]: Don't you use that—

TOM: —supposed to do!

AMANDA: —expression! Not in my—

TOM: Ohhh!

AMANDA: —presence! Have you gone out of your senses?

TOM: I have, that's true, *driven* out!

AMANDA: What is the matter with you, you—big—big—IDIOT!

TOM: Look!—I've got *no thing,* no single thing—

AMANDA: Lower your voice!

TOM: —in my life here that I can call my OWN! Everything is—

AMANDA: Stop that shouting!

TOM: Yesterday you confiscated my books! You had the nerve to—

AMANDA: I took that horrible novel back to the library—yes! That hideous book by that insane Mr. Lawrence.

[*Tom laughs wildly.*]

I cannot control the output of diseased minds or people who cater to them—

[*Tom laughs still more wildly.*]

BUT I WON'T ALLOW SUCH FILTH BROUGHT INTO MY HOUSE! No, no, no, no, no!

TOM: House, house! Who pays rent on it, who makes a slave of himself to—

AMANDA [*fairly screeching*]: Don't you DARE to—

TOM: No, no, *I* mustn't say things! *I've* got to just—

AMANDA: Let me tell you—

TOM: I don't want to hear any more!

[*He tears the portieres open. The dining-room area is lit with a turgid smoky red glow. Now we see Amanda; her hair is in metal curlers and she is wearing a very old bathrobe, much too large for her slight figure, a relic of the faithless Mr. Wingfield. The upright typewriter now stands on the drop-leaf table, along with a wild disarray of manuscripts. The quarrel was probably precipitated by Amanda's interruption of Tom's creative labor. A chair lies overthrown on the floor. Their gesticulating shadows are cast on the ceiling by the fiery glow.*]

AMANDA: You *will* hear more, you—

TOM: No, I won't hear more, I'm going out!

AMANDA: You come right back in—

TOM: Out, out, out! Because I'm—

AMANDA: Come back here, Tom Wingfield! I'm not through talking to you!

TOM: Oh, go—

LAURA [*desperately*]: —Tom!

AMANDA: You're going to listen, and no more insolence from you! I'm at the end of my patience!

[*He comes back toward her.*]

TOM: What do you think I'm at? Aren't I supposed to have any patience to reach the end of, Mother? I know, I know. It seems unimportant to you, what I'm *doing*—what I *want* to do—having a little *difference* between them! You don't think that—

AMANDA: I think you've been doing things that you're ashamed of. That's why you act like this. I don't believe that you go every night to the movies. Nobody goes to the movies night after night. Nobody in their right minds goes to the movies as often as you pretend to. People don't go to the movies at nearly midnight, and movies don't let out at two A.M. Come in stumbling. Muttering to yourself like a maniac! You get three hours' sleep and then go to work. Oh, I can picture the way you're doing down there. Moping, doping, because you're in no condition.

TOM [*wildly*]: No, I'm in no condition!

AMANDA: What right have you got to jeopardize your job? Jeopardize the security of us all? How do you think we'd manage if you were—

TOM: Listen! You think I'm crazy about the *warehouse?* [*He bends fiercely toward her slight figure.*] You think I'm in love with the Continental Shoemakers? You think I want to spend fifty-five *years* down there in that—*celotex interior!* with—*fluorescent—tubes!* Look! I'd rather somebody picked up a crowbar and battered out my brains—than go back mornings! I *go!* Every time you come in yelling that God-damn *"Rise and Shine!" "Rise and Shine!"* I say to myself, "How *lucky dead* people are!" But I get up. I *go!* For sixty-five dollars a month I give up all that I dream of doing and being *ever!* And you say self—*self's* all I ever think of. Why, listen, if self is what I thought of, Mother, I'd be where he is—GONE! [*He points to his father's picture.*] As far as the system of transportation reaches! [*He starts past her. She grabs his arm.*] Don't grab at me, Mother!

AMANDA: Where are you going?

TOM: I'm going to the *movies!*

AMANDA: I don't believe that lie!

[*Tom crouches toward her, overtowering her tiny figure. She backs away, gasping.*]

TOM: I'm going to opium dens! Yes, opium dens, dens of vice and criminals' hangouts, Mother. I've joined the Hogan Gang, I'm a hired assassin, I carry a tommy gun in a violin case! I run a string of cat houses in the Valley! They call me Killer, Killer Wingfield, I'm leading a double-life, a simple, honest warehouse worker by day, by night a dynamic *czar* of the *underworld, Mother.* I go to gambling casinos, I spin away fortunes on the roulette table! I wear a patch over one eye and a false mustache, sometimes I put on green whiskers. On those occasions they call me—*El Diablo!* Oh, I could tell you many things to make you sleepless! My enemies plan to dynamite this place. They're going to blow us all sky-high some night! I'll be glad, very happy, and so will you! You'll go up, up on a broomstick, over Blue Mountain with seventeen gentlemen callers! You ugly—babbling old—*witch*. . . . [*He goes through a series of violent, clumsy movements, seizing his overcoat, lunging to the door, pulling it fiercely open. The women watch him, aghast. His arm catches in the sleeve of the coat as he struggles to pull it on. For a moment he is pinioned by the bulky garment. With an outraged groan he tears the coat off again, splitting the shoulder of it, and hurls it across the room. It strikes against the shelf of Laura's glass collection, and there is a tinkle of shattering glass. Laura cries out as if wounded.*]

[*Music.*]

[*Screen legend*: "The Glass Menagerie."]

LAURA [*shrilly*]: *My glass!*—menagerie. . . . [*She covers her face and turns away.*]

[*But Amanda is still stunned and stupefied by the "ugly witch" so that she barely notices this occurrence. Now she recovers her speech.*]

AMANDA [*in an awful voice*]: I won't speak to you—until you apologize!

[*She crosses through the portieres and draws them together behind her. Tom is left with Laura. Laura clings weakly to the mantel with her face averted. Tom stares at her stupidly for a moment. Then he crosses to the shelf. He drops awkwardly on his knees to collect the fallen glass, glancing at Laura as if he would speak but couldn't.*]

[*"The Glass Menagerie" music steals in as the scene dims out.*]

SCENE FOUR

The interior of the apartment is dark. There is a faint light in the alley. A deep-voiced bell in a church is tolling the hour of five.

Tom appears at the top of the alley. After each solemn boom of the bell in the tower, he shakes a little noisemaker or rattle as if to express the tiny spasm of man in contrast to the sustained power and dignity of the Almighty. This and the unsteadiness of his advance make it evident that he has been drinking. As he climbs the few steps to the fire escape landing light steals up inside. Laura appears in the front room in a nightdress. She notices that Tom's bed is empty. Tom fishes in his pockets for his door key, removing a motley assortment of articles in the search, including a shower of movie ticket stubs and an empty bottle. At last he finds the key, but just as he is about to insert it, it slips from his fingers. He strikes a match and crouches below the door.

TOM [*bitterly*]: One crack—and it falls through!

[*Laura opens the door.*]

LAURA: Tom! Tom, what are you doing?

TOM: Looking for a door key.

LAURA: Where have you been all this time?

TOM: I have been to the movies.

LAURA: All this time at the movies?

TOM: There was a very long program. There was a Garbo picture and a Mickey Mouse and a travelogue and a newsreel and a preview of coming attractions. And there was an organ solo and a collection for the Milk Fund—simultaneously—

which ended up in a terrible fight between a fat lady and an usher!

LAURA [*innocently*]: Did you have to stay through everything?

TOM: Of course! And, oh, I forgot! There was a big stage show! The headliner on this stage show was Malvolio the Magician. He performed wonderful tricks, many of them, such as pouring water back and forth between pitchers. First it turned to wine and then it turned to beer and then it turned to whisky. I know it was whisky it finally turned into because he needed somebody to come up out of the audience to help him, and I came up—both shows! It was Kentucky Straight Bourbon. A very generous fellow, he gave souvenirs. [*He pulls from his back pocket a shimmering rainbow-colored scarf.*] He gave me this. This is his magic scarf. You can have it, Laura. You wave it over a canary cage and you get a bowl of goldfish. You wave it over the goldfish bowl and they fly away canaries. . . . But the wonderfullest trick of all was the coffin trick. We nailed him into a coffin and he got out of the coffin without removing one nail. [*He has come inside.*] There is a trick that would come in handy for me—get me out of this two-by-four situation! [*He flops onto the bed and starts removing his shoes.*]

LAURA: Tom—shhh!

TOM: What're you shushing me for?

LAURA: You'll wake up Mother.

TOM: Goody, goody! Pay 'er back for all those "Rise an' Shines." [*He lies down, groaning.*] You know it don't take much intelligence to get yourself into a nailed-up coffin, Laura. But who in hell ever got himself out of one without removing one nail?

[*As if in answer, the father's grinning photograph lights up. The scene dims out.*]

[*Immediately following, the church bell is heard striking six. At the sixth stroke the alarm clock goes off in Amanda's room, and after a few moments we hear her calling: "Rise and Shine! Rise and Shine! Laura, go tell your brother to rise and shine!"*]

TOM [*sitting up slowly*]: I'll rise—but I won't shine.

[*The light increases.*]

AMANDA: Laura, tell your brother his coffee is ready.

[*Laura slips into the front room.*]

LAURA: Tom!—It's nearly seven. Don't make Mother nervous.

[*He stares at her stupidly.*]

[*beseechingly:*] Tom, speak to Mother this morning. Make up with her, apologize, speak to her!

TOM: She won't to me. It's her that started not speaking.

LAURA: If you just say you're sorry she'll start speaking.

TOM: Her not speaking—is that such a tragedy?

LAURA: Please—please!

AMANDA [*calling from the kitchenette*]: Laura, are you going to do what I asked you to do, or do I have to get dressed and go out myself?

LAURA: Going, going—soon as I get on my coat!

[*She pulls on a shapeless felt hat with a nervous, jerky movement, pleadingly glancing at Tom. She rushes awk-*

wardly for her coat. The coat is one of Amanda's, inaccurately made-over, the sleeves too short for Laura.]

Butter and what else?

AMANDA [*entering from the kitchenette*]: Just butter. Tell them to charge it.

LAURA: Mother, they make such faces when I do that.

AMANDA: Sticks and stones can break our bones, but the expression on Mr. Garfinkel's face won't harm us! Tell your brother his coffee is getting cold.

LAURA [*at the door*]: Do what I asked you, will you, will you, Tom?

[*He looks sullenly away.*]

AMANDA: Laura, go now or just don't go at all!

LAURA [*rushing out*]: Going—going!

[*A second later she cries out. Tom springs up and crosses to the door. Tom opens the door.*]

TOM: Laura?

LAURA: I'm all right. I slipped, but I'm all right.

AMANDA [*peering anxiously after her*]: If anyone breaks a leg on those fire-escape steps, the landlord ought to be sued for every cent he possesses! [*She shuts the door. Now she remembers she isn't speaking to Tom and returns to the other room.*]

[*As Tom comes listlessly for his coffee, she turns her back to him and stands rigidly facing the window on the gloomy gray vault of the areaway. Its light on her face with its aged but childish features is cruelly sharp, satirical as a Daumier print.*]

[*The music of "Ave Maria," is heard softly.*]

[*Tom glances sheepishly but sullenly at her averted figure and slumps at the table. The coffee is scalding hot; he sips it and gasps and spits it back in the cup. At his gasp, Amanda catches her breath and half turns. Then she catches herself and turns back to the window. Tom blows on his coffee, glancing sidewise at his mother. She clears her throat. Tom clears his. He starts to rise, sinks back down again, scratches his head, clears his throat again. Amanda coughs. Tom raises his cup in both hands to blow on it, his eyes staring over the rim of it at his mother for several moments. Then he slowly sets the cup down and awkwardly and hesitantly rises from the chair.*]

TOM [*hoarsely*]: Mother. I—I apologize, Mother.

[*Amanda draws a quick, shuddering breath. Her face works grotesquely. She breaks into childlike tears.*]

I'm sorry for what I said, for everything that I said, I didn't mean it.

AMANDA [*sobbingly*]: My devotion has made me a witch and so I make myself hateful to my children!

TOM: *No,* you *don't.*

AMANDA: I worry so much, don't sleep, it makes me nervous!

TOM [*gently*]: I understand that.

AMANDA: I've had to put up a solitary battle all these years. But you're my right-hand bower! Don't fall down, don't fail!

TOM [*gently*]: I try, Mother.

AMANDA [*with great enthusiasm*]: Try and you will *succeed!* [*The notion makes her breathless.*] Why, you—you're just *full* of natural endowments! Both of my children—they're *unusual* children! Don't you think I know it? I'm so—*proud!* Happy and—feel I've—so much to be thankful for but— promise me one thing, son!

TOM: What, Mother?

AMANDA: Promise, son, you'll—never be a drunkard!

TOM [*turns to her grinning*]: I will never be a drunkard, Mother.

AMANDA: That's what frightened me so, that you'd be drinking! Eat a bowl of Purina!

TOM: Just coffee, Mother.

AMANDA: Shredded wheat biscuit?

TOM: No. No, Mother, just coffee.

AMANDA: You can't put in a day's work on an empty stomach. You've got ten minutes—don't gulp! Drinking too-hot liquids makes cancer of the stomach. . . . Put cream in.

TOM: No, thank you.

AMANDA: To cool it.

TOM: No! No, thank you, I want it black.

AMANDA: I know, but it's not good for you. We have to do all that we can to build ourselves up. In these trying times we live in, all that we have to cling to is—each other. . . . That's why it's so important to— Tom, I— I sent out your sister so I could discuss something with you. If you hadn't spoken I would have spoken to you. [*She sits down.*]

TOM [*gently*]: What is it, Mother, that you want to discuss?

AMANDA: *Laura!*

[*Tom puts his cup down slowly.*]

[*Legend on screen*: "Laura." *Music*: *"The Glass Menagerie."*]

TOM: —Oh.—Laura . . .

AMANDA [*touching his sleeve*]: You know how Laura is. So quiet but—still water runs deep! She notices things and I think she—broods about them.

[*Tom looks up.*]

A few days ago I came in and she was crying.

TOM: What about?

AMANDA: You.

TOM: Me?

AMANDA: She has an idea that you're not happy here.

TOM: What gave her that idea?

AMANDA: What gives her any idea? However, you do act strangely. I—I'm not criticizing, understand *that!* I know your ambitions do not lie in the warehouse, that like everybody in the whole wide world—you've had to—make sacrifices, but—Tom—Tom—life's not easy, it calls for—Spartan endurance! There's so many things in my heart that I cannot describe to you! I've never told you but I—*loved* your father. . . .

TOM [*gently*]: I know that, Mother.

AMANDA: And you—when I see you taking after his ways! Staying out late—and—well, you *had* been drinking the night you were in that—terrifying condition! Laura says that you hate the apartment and that you go out nights to get away from it! Is that true, Tom?

TOM: No. You say there's so much in your heart that you can't describe to me. That's true of me, too. There's so much in my heart that I can't describe to *you!* So let's respect each other's—

AMANDA: But, why—*why*, Tom—are you always so *restless?* Where do you *go* to, nights?

TOM: I—go to the movies.

AMANDA: Why do you go to the movies so much, Tom?

TOM: I go to the movies because—I like adventure. Adventure is something I don't have much of at work, so I go to the movies.

AMANDA: But, Tom, you go to the movies *entirely* too *much!*

TOM: I like a lot of adventure.

[*Amanda looks baffled, then hurt. As the familiar inquisition resumes, Tom becomes hard and impatient again. Amanda slips back into her querulous attitude toward him.*]

[*Image on screen*: A sailing vessel with Jolly Roger.]

AMANDA: Most young men find adventure in their careers.

TOM: Then most young men are not employed in a warehouse.

AMANDA: The world is full of young men employed in warehouses and offices and factories.

TOM: Do all of them find adventure in their careers?

AMANDA: They do or they do without it! Not everybody has a craze for adventure.

TOM: Man is by instinct a lover, a hunter, a fighter, and none of those instincts are given much play at the warehouse!

AMANDA: Man is by instinct! Don't quote instinct to me! Instinct is something that people have got away from! It belongs to animals! Christian adults don't want it!

TOM: What do Christian adults want, then, Mother?

AMANDA: Superior things! Things of the mind and the spirit! Only animals have to satisfy instincts! Surely your aims are somewhat higher than theirs! Than monkeys—pigs—

TOM: I reckon they're not.

AMANDA: You're joking. However, that isn't what I wanted to discuss.

TOM [*rising*]: I haven't much time.

AMANDA [*pushing his shoulders*]: Sit down.

TOM: You want me to punch in red at the warehouse, Mother?

AMANDA: You have five minutes. I want to talk about Laura.

[*Screen legend*: "Plans and Provisions."]

TOM: All right! What about Laura?

AMANDA: We have to be making some plans and provisions for her. She's older than you, two years, and nothing has happened. She just drifts along doing nothing. It frightens me terribly how she just drifts along.

TOM: I guess she's the type that people call home girls.

AMANDA: There's no such type, and if there is, it's a pity! That is unless the home is hers, with a husband!

TOM: What?

AMANDA: Oh, I can see the handwriting on the wall as plain as I see the nose in front of my face! It's terrifying! More and more you remind me of your father! He was out all hours without explanation!—Then *left! Goodbye!* And me with the bag to hold. I saw that letter you got from the Merchant Marine. I know what you're dreaming of. I'm not standing here blindfolded. [*She pauses.*] Very well, then. Then *do* it! But not till there's somebody to take your place.

TOM: What do you mean?

AMANDA: I mean that as soon as Laura has got somebody to take care of her, married, a home of her own, independent—why, then you'll be free to go wherever you please, on land, on sea, whichever way the wind blows you! But until that time you've got to look out for your sister. I don't say me because I'm old and don't matter! I say for your sister because she's young and dependent.

I put her in business college—a dismal failure! Frightened her so it made her sick at the stomach. I took her over to the Young People's League at the church. Another fiasco. She spoke to nobody, nobody spoke to her. Now all she does is fool with those pieces of glass and play those worn-out records. What kind of a life is that for a girl to lead?

TOM: What can I do about it?

AMANDA: Overcome selfishness! Self, self, self is all that you ever think of!

[*Tom springs up and crosses to get his coat. It is ugly and bulky. He pulls on a cap with earmuffs.*]

Where is your muffler? Put your wool muffler on!

[*He snatches it angrily from the closet, tosses it around his neck and pulls both ends tight.*]

Tom! I haven't said what I had in mind to ask you.

TOM: I'm too late to—

AMANDA [*catching his arm—very importunately; then shyly*]: Down at the warehouse, aren't there some—nice young men?

TOM: No!

AMANDA: There *must* be—*some* . . .

TOM: Mother—[*He gestures.*]

AMANDA: Find out one that's clean-living—doesn't drink and ask him out for sister!

TOM: What?

AMANDA: For *sister!* To *meet!* Get *acquainted!*

TOM [*stamping to the door*]: Oh, my *go-osh!*

AMANDA: Will you?

[*He opens the door. She says, imploringly:*]

Will you?

[*He starts down the fire escape.*]

Will you? *Will* you, dear?

TOM [*calling back*]: *Yes!*

[*Amanda closes the door hesitantly and with a troubled but faintly hopeful expression.*]

[*Screen image*: The cover of a glamor magazine.]

[*The spotlight picks up Amanda at the phone.*]

AMANDA: Ella Cartwright? This is Amanda Wingfield!
How are you, honey?
How is that kidney condition?

[*There is a five-second pause.*]

Horrors!

[*There is another pause.*]

You're a Christian martyr, yes, honey, that's what you are, a Christian martyr! Well, I just now happened to notice in my little red book that your subscription to the *Companion* has just run out! I knew that you wouldn't want to miss out on the wonderful serial starting in this new issue. It's by Bessie Mae Hopper, the first thing she's written since *Honeymoon for Three*. Wasn't that a strange and interesting story? Well, this one is even lovelier, I believe. It has a sophisticated, society background. It's all about the horsey set on Long Island!

[*The light fades out.*]

SCENE FIVE

Legend on the screen: "Annunciation."

Music is heard as the light slowly comes on.

It is early dusk of a spring evening. Supper has just been finished in the Wingfield apartment. Amanda and Laura, in light-colored dresses, are removing dishes from the table in the dining room, which is shadowy, their movements formalized almost as a dance or ritual, their moving forms as pale and silent as moths. Tom, in white shirt and trousers, rises from the table and crosses toward the fire escape.

AMANDA [*as he passes her*]: Son, will you do me a favor?

TOM: What?

AMANDA: Comb your hair! You look so pretty when your hair is combed!

[*Tom slouches on the sofa with the evening paper. Its enormous headline reads: "Franco Triumphs."*]

There is only one respect in which I would like you to emulate your father.

TOM: What respect is that?

AMANDA: The care he always took of his appearance. He never allowed himself to look untidy.

[*He throws down the paper and crosses to the fire escape.*]

Where are you going?

TOM: I'm going out to smoke.

AMANDA: You smoke too much. A pack a day at fifteen cents a pack. How much would that amount to in a month?

Thirty times fifteen is how much, Tom? Figure it out and you will be astounded at what you could save. Enough to give you a night-school course in accounting at Washington U.! Just think what a wonderful thing that would be for you, son!

[*Tom is unmoved by the thought.*]

TOM: I'd rather smoke. [*He steps out on the landing, letting the screen door slam.*]

AMANDA [*sharply*]: I know! That's the tragedy of it. . . . [*Alone, she turns to look at her husband's picture.*]

[*Dance music: "The World Is Waiting for the Sunrise!"*]

TOM [*to the audience*]: Across the alley from us was the Paradise Dance Hall. On evenings in spring the windows and doors were open and the music came outdoors. Sometimes the lights were turned out except for a large glass sphere that hung from the ceiling. It would turn slowly about and filter the dusk with delicate rainbow colors. Then the orchestra played a waltz or a tango, something that had a slow and sensuous rhythm. Couples would come outside, to the relative privacy of the alley. You could see them kissing behind ash pits and telephone poles. This was the compensation for lives that passed like mine, without any change or adventure. Adventure and change were imminent in this year. They were waiting around the corner for all these kids. Suspended in the mist over Berchtesgaden, caught in the folds of Chamberlain's umbrella. In Spain there was Guernica! But here there was only hot swing music and liquor, dance halls, bars, and movies, and sex that hung in the gloom like a chandelier and flooded the world with brief, deceptive rainbows. . . . All the world was waiting for bombardments!

[*Amanda turns from the picture and comes outside.*]

AMANDA [*sighing*]: A fire escape landing's a poor excuse for a porch. [*She spreads a newspaper on a step and sits down, gracefully and demurely as if she were settling into a swing on a Mississippi veranda.*] What are you looking at?

TOM: The moon.

AMANDA: Is there a moon this evening?

TOM: It's rising over Garfinkel's Delicatessen.

AMANDA: So it is! A little silver slipper of a moon. Have you made a wish on it yet?

TOM: Um-hum.

AMANDA: What did you wish for?

TOM: That's a secret.

AMANDA: A secret, huh? Well, I won't tell mine either. I will be just as mysterious as you.

TOM: I bet I can guess what yours is.

AMANDA: Is my head so transparent?

TOM: You're not a sphinx.

AMANDA: No, I don't have secrets. I'll tell you what I wished for on the moon. Success and happiness for my precious children! I wish for that whenever there's a moon, and when there isn't a moon, I wish for it, too.

TOM: I thought perhaps you wished for a gentleman caller.

AMANDA: Why do you say that?

TOM: Don't you remember asking me to fetch one?

AMANDA: I remember suggesting that it would be nice for your sister if you brought home some nice young man from the warehouse. I think that I've made that suggestion more than once.

TOM: Yes, you have made it repeatedly.

AMANDA: Well?

TOM: We are going to have one.

AMANDA: *What?*

TOM: A gentleman caller!

[*The annunciation is celebrated with music.*]

[*Amanda rises.*]

[*Image on screen*: A caller with a bouquet.]

AMANDA: You mean you have asked some nice young man to come over?

TOM: Yep. I've asked him to dinner.

AMANDA: You really did?

TOM: I did!

AMANDA: You did, and did he—*accept?*

TOM: He did!

AMANDA: Well, well—well, well! That's—lovely!

TOM: I thought that you would be pleased.

AMANDA: It's definite then?

TOM: Very definite.

AMANDA: Soon?

TOM: Very soon.

AMANDA: For heaven's sake, stop putting on and tell me some things, will you?

TOM: What things do you want me to tell you?

AMANDA: *Naturally* I would like to know when he's *coming!*

TOM: He's coming tomorrow.

AMANDA: *Tomorrow?*

TOM: Yep. Tomorrow.

AMANDA: But, Tom!

TOM: Yes, Mother?

AMANDA: Tomorrow gives me no time!

TOM: Time for what?

AMANDA: Preparations! Why didn't you phone me at once, as soon as you asked him, the minute that he accepted? Then, don't you see, I could have been getting ready!

TOM: You don't have to make any fuss.

AMANDA: Oh, Tom, Tom, Tom, of course I have to make a fuss! I want things nice, not sloppy! Not thrown together. I'll certainly have to do some fast thinking, won't I?

TOM: I don't see why you have to think at all.

AMANDA: You just don't know. We can't have a gentleman caller in a pigsty! All my wedding silver has to be polished, the monogrammed table linen ought to be laundered! The windows have to be washed and fresh curtains put up. And how about clothes? We have to *wear* something, don't we?

TOM: Mother, this boy is no one to make a fuss over!

AMANDA: Do you realize he's the first young man we've introduced to your sister? It's terrible, dreadful, disgraceful that poor little sister has never received a single gentleman caller! Tom, come inside! [*She opens the screen door.*]

TOM: What for?

AMANDA: I want to ask you some things.

TOM: If you're going to make such a fuss, I'll call it off, I'll tell him not to come!

AMANDA: You certainly won't do anything of the kind. Nothing offends people worse than broken engagements. It simply means I'll have to work like a Turk! We won't be brilliant, but we will pass inspection. Come on inside.

[*Tom follows her inside, groaning.*]

Sit down.

TOM: Any particular place you would like me to sit?

AMANDA: Thank heavens I've got that new sofa! I'm also making payments on a floor lamp I'll have sent out! And put the chintz covers on, they'll brighten things up! Of course I'd hoped to have these walls re-papered. . . . What is the young man's name?

TOM: His name is O'Connor.

AMANDA: That, of course, means fish—tomorrow is Friday! I'll have that salmon loaf—with Durkee's dressing! What does he do? He works at the warehouse?

TOM: Of course! How else would I—

AMANDA: Tom, he—doesn't drink?

TOM: Why do you ask me that?

AMANDA: Your father *did!*

TOM: Don't get started on that!

AMANDA: He *does* drink, then?

TOM: Not that I know of!

AMANDA: Make sure, be certain! The last thing I want for my daughter's a boy who drinks!

TOM: Aren't you being a little bit premature? Mr. O'Connor has not yet appeared on the scene!

AMANDA: But will tomorrow. To meet your sister, and what do I know about his character? Nothing! Old maids are better off than wives of drunkards!

TOM: Oh, my God!

AMANDA: Be still!

TOM [*leaning forward to whisper*]: Lots of fellows meet girls whom they don't marry!

AMANDA: Oh, talk sensibly, Tom—and don't be sarcastic! [*She has gotten a hairbrush.*]

TOM: What are you doing?

AMANDA: I'm brushing that cowlick down! [*She attacks his hair with the brush.*] What is this young man's position at the warehouse?

TOM [*submitting grimly to the brush and the interrogation*]: This young man's position is that of a shipping clerk, Mother.

AMANDA: Sounds to me like a fairly responsible job, the sort of a job *you* would be in if you just had more *get-up*. What is his salary? Have you any idea?

TOM: I would judge it to be approximately eighty-five dollars a month.

AMANDA: Well—not princely, but—

TOM: Twenty more than I make.

AMANDA: Yes, how well I know! But for a family man, eighty-five dollars a month is not much more than you can just get by on. . . .

TOM: Yes, but Mr. O'Connor is not a family man.

AMANDA: He might be, mightn't he? Some time in the future?

TOM: I see. Plans and provisions.

AMANDA: You are the only young man that I know of who ignores the fact that the future becomes the present, the present the past, and the past turns into everlasting regret if you don't plan for it!

TOM: I will think that over and see what I can make of it.

AMANDA: Don't be supercilious with your mother! Tell me some more about this—what do you call him?

TOM: James D. O'Connor. The D. is for Delaney.

AMANDA: Irish on *both* sides! *Gracious!* And doesn't drink?

TOM: Shall I call him up and ask him right this minute?

AMANDA: The only way to find out about those things is to make discreet inquiries at the proper moment. When I was a girl in Blue Mountain and it was suspected that a young man drank, the girl whose attentions he had been receiving, if any girl *was*, would sometimes speak to the minister of his church, or rather her father would if her father was living, and sort of feel him out on the young man's character. That is the way such things are discreetly handled to keep a young woman from making a tragic mistake!

TOM: Then how did you happen to make a tragic mistake?

AMANDA: That innocent look of your father's had everyone fooled! He *smiled*—the world was *enchanted!* No girl can do worse than put herself at the mercy of a handsome appearance! I hope that Mr. O'Connor is not too good-looking.

TOM: No, he's not too good-looking. He's covered with freckles and hasn't too much of a nose.

AMANDA: He's not right-down homely, though?

TOM: Not right-down homely. Just medium homely, I'd say.

AMANDA: Character's what to look for in a man.

TOM: That's what I've always said, Mother.

AMANDA: You've never said anything of the kind and I suspect you would never give it a thought.

TOM: Don't be so suspicious of me.

AMANDA: At least I hope he's the type that's up and coming.

TOM: I think he really goes in for self-improvement.

AMANDA: What reason have you to think so?

TOM: He goes to night school.

AMANDA [*beaming*]: Splendid! What does he do, I mean study?

TOM: Radio engineering and public speaking!

AMANDA: Then he has visions of being advanced in the world! Any young man who studies public speaking is aiming to have an executive job some day! And radio engineering? A thing for the future! Both of these facts are very illuminating. Those are the sort of things that a mother should know concerning any young man who comes to call on her daughter. Seriously or—not.

TOM: One little warning. He doesn't know about Laura. I didn't let on that we had dark ulterior motives. I just said, why don't you come and have dinner with us? He said okay and that was the whole conversation.

AMANDA: I bet it was! You're eloquent as an oyster. However, he'll know about Laura when he gets here. When he sees how lovely and sweet and pretty she is, he'll thank his lucky stars he was asked to dinner.

TOM: Mother, you mustn't expect too much of Laura.

AMANDA: What do you mean?

TOM: Laura seems all those things to you and me because she's ours and we love her. We don't even notice she's crippled any more.

AMANDA: Don't say crippled! You know that I never allow that word to be used!

TOM: But face facts, Mother. She is and—that's not all—

AMANDA: What do you mean "not all"?

TOM: Laura is very different from other girls.

AMANDA: I think the difference is all to her advantage.

TOM: Not quite all—in the eyes of others—strangers—she's terribly shy and lives in a world of her own and those things make her seem a little peculiar to people outside the house.

AMANDA: Don't say peculiar.

TOM: Face the facts. She is.

[*The dance hall music changes to a tango that has a minor and somewhat ominous tone.*]

AMANDA: In what way is she peculiar—may I ask?

TOM [*gently*]: She lives in a world of her own—a world of little glass ornaments, Mother. . . .

[*He gets up. Amanda remains holding the brush, looking at him, troubled.*]

She plays old phonograph records and—that's about all—[*He glances at himself in the mirror and crosses to the door.*]

AMANDA [*sharply*]: Where are you going?

TOM: I'm going to the movies. [*He goes out the screen door.*]

AMANDA: Not to the movies, every night to the movies! [*She follows quickly to the screen door.*] I don't believe you always go to the movies!

[*He is gone. Amanda looks worriedly after him for a moment. Then vitality and optimism return and she turns from the door, crossing to the portieres.*]

Laura! Laura!

[*Laura answers from the kitchenette.*]

LAURA: Yes, Mother.

AMANDA: Let those dishes go and come in front!

[*Laura appears with a dish towel. Amanda speaks to her gaily.*]

Laura, come here and make a wish on the moon!

[*Screen image*: The Moon.]

LAURA [*entering*]: Moon—moon?

AMANDA: A little silver slipper of a moon. Look over your left shoulder, Laura, and make a wish!

[*Laura looks faintly puzzled as if called out of sleep. Amanda seizes her shoulders and turns her at an angle by the door.*]

Now! Now, darling, *wish!*

LAURA: What shall I wish for, Mother?

AMANDA [*her voice trembling and her eyes suddenly filling with tears*]: Happiness! Good fortune!

[*The sound of the violin rises and the stage dims out.*]

SCENE SIX

The light comes up on the fire escape landing. Tom is leaning against the grill, smoking.

[*Screen image*: The high school hero.]

TOM: And so the following evening I brought Jim home to dinner. I had known Jim slightly in high school. In high school Jim was a hero. He had tremendous Irish good nature and vitality with the scrubbed and polished look of white chinaware. He seemed to move in a continual spotlight. He was a star in basketball, captain of the debating club, president of the senior class and the glee club and he sang the male lead in the annual light operas. He was always running or bounding, never just walking. He seemed always at the point of defeating the law of gravity. He was shooting with such velocity through his adolescence that you would logically expect him to arrive at nothing short of the White House by the time he was thirty. But Jim apparently ran into more interference after his graduation from Soldan. His speed had definitely slowed. Six years after he left high school he was holding a job that wasn't much better than mine.

[*Screen image*: The Clerk.]

He was the only one at the warehouse with whom I was on friendly terms. I was valuable to him as someone who could remember his former glory, who had seen him win basketball games and the silver cup in debating. He knew of my secret practice of retiring to a cabinet of the washroom to work on poems when business was slack in the warehouse. He called me Shakespeare. And while the other boys in the warehouse regarded me with suspicious hostility, Jim took a humorous attitude toward me. Gradually his attitude affected the others, their hostility wore off and they also began to smile at me as people smile at an oddly fashioned dog who trots across their path at some distance.

I knew that Jim and Laura had known each other at Soldan, and I had heard Laura speak admiringly of his voice. I didn't know if Jim remembered her or not. In high school Laura had been as unobtrusive as Jim had been astonishing. If he did remember Laura, it was not as my sister, for when I asked him to dinner, he grinned and said, "You know, Shakespeare, I never thought of you as having folks!"

He was about to discover that I did. . . .

[*Legend on screen*: "The accent of a coming foot."]

[*The light dims out on Tom and comes up in the Wingfield living room—a delicate lemony light. It is about five on a Friday evening of late spring which comes "scattering poems in the sky."*]

[*Amanda has worked like a Turk in preparation for the gentleman caller. The results are astonishing. The new floor lamp with its rose silk shade is in place, a colored paper lantern conceals the broken light fixture in the ceiling, new billowing white curtains are at the windows, chintz covers are on the chairs and sofa, a pair of new sofa pillows make their initial appearance. Open boxes and tissue paper are scattered on the floor.*]

[*Laura stands in the middle of the room with lifted arms while Amanda crouches before her, adjusting the hem of a new dress, devout and ritualistic. The dress is colored and designed by memory. The arrangement of Laura's hair is changed; it is softer and more becoming. A fragile, unearthly prettiness has come out in Laura: she is like a piece of translucent glass touched by light, given a momentary radiance, not actual, not lasting.*]

AMANDA [*impatiently*]: Why are you trembling?

LAURA: Mother, you've made me so nervous!

AMANDA: How have I made you nervous?

LAURA: By all this fuss! You make it seem so important!

AMANDA: I don't understand you, Laura. You couldn't be satisfied with just sitting home, and yet whenever I try to arrange something for you, you seem to resist it. [*She gets up.*] Now take a look at yourself. No, wait! Wait just a moment—I have an idea!

LAURA: What is it now?

[*Amanda produces two powder puffs which she wraps in handkerchiefs and stuffs in Laura's bosom.*]

LAURA: Mother, what are you doing?

AMANDA: They call them "Gay Deceivers"!

LAURA: I won't wear them!

AMANDA: You will!

LAURA: Why should I?

AMANDA: Because, to be painfully honest, your chest is flat.

LAURA: You make it seem like we were setting a trap.

AMANDA: All pretty girls are a trap, a pretty trap, and men expect them to be.

[*Legend on screen*: "A pretty trap."]

Now look at yourself, young lady. This is the prettiest you will ever be! [*She stands back to admire Laura.*] I've got to fix myself now! You're going to be surprised by your mother's appearance!

[*Amanda crosses through the portieres, humming gaily. Laura moves slowly to the long mirror and stares solemnly at herself. A wind blows the white curtains inward in a slow, graceful motion and with a faint, sorrowful sighing.*]

AMANDA [*from somewhere behind the portieres*]: It isn't dark enough yet.

[*Laura turns slowly before the mirror with a troubled look.*]

[*Legend on screen*: "This is my sister: Celebrate her with strings!" *Music plays.*]

AMANDA [*laughing, still not visible*]: I'm going to show you something. I'm going to make a spectacular appearance!

LAURA: What is it, Mother?

AMANDA: Possess your soul in patience—you will see! Something I've resurrected from that old trunk! Styles haven't changed so terribly much after all. . . . [*She parts the portieres.*] Now just look at your mother! [*She wears a girlish frock of yellowed voile with a blue silk sash. She carries a bunch of jonquils—the legend of her youth is nearly revived. Now she speaks feverishly:*] This is the dress in which I led the cotillion. Won the cakewalk twice at Sunset Hill, wore one Spring to the Governor's Ball in Jackson! See how I sashayed around the ballroom, Laura? [*She raises her skirt and does a mincing step around the room.*] I wore it on Sundays for my gentlemen callers! I had it on the day I met your father. . . . I had malaria fever all that Spring. The change of climate from East Tennessee to the Delta—weakened resistance. I had a little temperature all the time—not enough to be serious—just enough to make me restless and giddy! Invitations poured in—parties all over the Delta! "Stay in bed," said Mother, "you have a fever!"—but I just wouldn't. I took quinine but kept on going, going! Evenings, dances!

Afternoons, long, long rides! Picnics—lovely! So lovely, that country in May—all lacy with dogwood, literally flooded with jonquils! That was the spring I had the craze for jonquils. Jonquils became an absolute obsession. Mother said, "Honey, there's no more room for jonquils." And still I kept on bringing in more jonquils. Whenever, wherever I saw them, I'd say, "Stop! Stop! I see jonquils!" I made the young men help me gather the jonquils! It was a joke, Amanda and her jonquils. Finally there were no more vases to hold them, every available space was filled with jonquils. No vases to hold them? All right, I'll hold them myself! And then I—[*She stops in front of the picture. Music plays.*] met your father! Malaria fever and jonquils and then—this—boy. . . . [*She switches on the rose-colored lamp.*] I hope they get here before it starts to rain. [*She crosses the room and places the jonquils in a bowl on the table.*] I gave your brother a little extra change so he and Mr. O'Connor could take the service car home.

LAURA [*with an altered look*]: What did you say his name was?

AMANDA: O'Connor.

LAURA: What is his first name?

AMANDA: I don't remember. Oh, yes, I do. It was—Jim!

[*Laura sways slightly and catches hold of a chair.*]

[*Legend on screen*: "Not Jim!"]

LAURA [*faintly*]: Not—Jim!

AMANDA: Yes, that was it, it was Jim! I've never known a Jim that wasn't nice!

[*The music becomes ominous.*]

LAURA: Are you sure his name is Jim O'Connor?

AMANDA: Yes. Why?

LAURA: Is he the one that Tom used to know in high school?

AMANDA: He didn't say so. I think he just got to know him at the warehouse.

LAURA: There was a Jim O'Connor we both knew in high school—[*then, with effort*] If that is the one that Tom is bringing to dinner—you'll have to excuse me, I won't come to the table.

AMANDA: What sort of nonsense is this?

LAURA: You asked me once if I'd ever liked a boy. Don't you remember I showed you this boy's picture?

AMANDA: You mean the boy you showed me in the yearbook?

LAURA: Yes, that boy.

AMANDA: Laura, Laura, were you in love with that boy?

LAURA: I don't know, Mother. All I know is I couldn't sit at the table if it was him!

AMANDA: It won't be him! It isn't the least bit likely. But whether it is or not, you will come to the table. You will not be excused.

LAURA: I'll have to be, Mother.

AMANDA: I don't intend to humor your silliness, Laura. I've had too much from you and your brother, both! So just sit down and compose yourself till they come. Tom has forgotten his key so you'll have to let them in, when they arrive.

LAURA [*panicky*]: Oh, Mother—*you* answer the door!

AMANDA [*lightly*]: I'll be in the kitchen—busy!

LAURA: Oh, Mother, please answer the door, don't make me do it!

AMANDA [*crossing into the kitchenette*]: I've got to fix the dressing for the salmon. Fuss, fuss—silliness!—over a gentleman caller!

[*The door swings shut. Laura is left alone.*]

[*Legend on screen*: "Terror!"]

[*She utters a low moan and turns off the lamp—sits stiffly on the edge of the sofa, knotting her fingers together.*]

[*Legend on screen*: "The Opening of a Door!"]

[*Tom and Jim appear on the fire escape steps and climb to the landing. Hearing their approach, Laura rises with a panicky gesture. She retreats to the portieres. The doorbell rings. Laura catches her breath and touches her throat. Low drums sound.*]

AMANDA [*calling*]: Laura, sweetheart! The door!

[*Laura stares at it without moving.*]

JIM: I think we just beat the rain.

TOM: Uh-huh. [*He rings again, nervously. Jim whistles and fishes for a cigarette.*]

AMANDA [*very, very gaily*]: Laura, that is your brother and Mr. O'Connor! Will you let them in, darling?

[*Laura crosses toward the kitchenette door.*]

LAURA [*breathlessly*]: Mother—you go to the door!

Amanda steps out of the kitchenette and stares furiously at Laura. She points imperiously at the door.]

LAURA: Please, please!

AMANDA [*in a fierce whisper*]: What is the matter with you, you silly thing?

LAURA [*desperately*]: Please, you answer it, *please!*

AMANDA: I told you I wasn't going to humor you, Laura. Why have you chosen this moment to lose your mind?

LAURA: Please, please, please, you go!

AMANDA: You'll have to go to the door because I can't!

LAURA [*despairingly*]: I can't either!

AMANDA: *Why?*

LAURA: I'm *sick!*

AMANDA: I'm sick, too—of your nonsense! Why can't you and your brother be normal people? Fantastic whims and behavior!

[*Tom gives a long ring.*]

Preposterous goings on! Can you give me one reason—[*She calls out lyrically.*] *Coming! Just one second!*—why you should be afraid to open a door? Now you answer it, Laura!

LAURA: Oh, oh, oh . . . [*She returns through the portieres, darts to the Victrola, winds it frantically and turns it on.*]

AMANDA: Laura Wingfield, you march right to that door!

LAURA: *Yes—yes, Mother!*

[*A faraway, scratchy rendition of "Dardanella" softens the air and gives her strength to move through it. She slips to the door and draws it cautiously open. Tom enters with the caller, Jim O'Connor.*]

TOM: Laura, this is Jim. Jim, this is my sister, Laura.

JIM [*stepping inside*]: I didn't know that Shakespeare had a sister!

LAURA [*retreating, stiff and trembling, from the door*]: How—how do you do?

JIM [*heartily, extending his hand*]: Okay!

[*Laura touches it hesitantly with hers.*]

JIM: Your hand's *cold,* Laura!

LAURA: Yes, well—I've been playing the Victrola. . . .

JIM: Must have been playing classical music on it! You ought to play a little hot swing music to warm you up!

LAURA: Excuse me—I haven't finished playing the Victrola. . . . [*She turns awkwardly and hurries into the front room. She pauses a second by the Victrola. Then she catches her breath and darts through the portieres like a frightened deer.*]

JIM [*grinning*]: What was the matter?

TOM: Oh—with Laura? Laura is—terribly shy.

JIM: Shy, huh? It's unusual to meet a shy girl nowadays. I don't believe you ever mentioned you had a sister.

TOM: Well, now you know. I have one. Here is the *Post Dispatch.* You want a piece of it?

JIM: Uh-huh.

TOM: What piece? The comics?

JIM: Sports! [*He glances at it.*] Ole Dizzy Dean is on his bad behavior.

TOM [*uninterested*]: Yeah? [*He lights a cigarette and goes over to the fire-escape door.*]

JIM: Where are *you* going?

TOM: I'm going out on the terrace.

JIM [*going after him*]: You know, Shakespeare—I'm going to sell you a bill of goods!

TOM: What goods?

JIM: A course I'm taking.

TOM: Huh?

JIM: In public speaking! You and me, we're not the warehouse type.

TOM: Thanks—that's good news. But what has public speaking got to do with it?

JIM: It fits you for—executive positions!

TOM: Awww.

JIM: I tell you it's done a helluva lot for me.

[*Image on screen*: Executive at his desk.]

TOM: In what respect?

JIM: In every! Ask yourself what is the difference between you an' me and men in the office down front? Brains?—No! —Ability?—No! Then what? Just one little thing—

TOM: What is that one little thing?

JIM: Primarily it amounts to—social poise! Being able to square up to people and hold your own on any social level!

AMANDA [*from the kitchenette*]:Tom?

TOM: Yes, Mother?

AMANDA: Is that you and Mr. O'Connor?

TOM: Yes, Mother.

AMANDA: Well, you just make yourselves comfortable in there.

TOM: Yes, Mother.

AMANDA: Ask Mr. O'Connor if he would like to wash his hands.

JIM: Aw, no—no—thank you—I took care of that at the warehouse. Tom—

TOM: Yes?

JIM: Mr. Mendoza was speaking to me about you.

TOM: Favorably?

JIM: What do you think?

TOM: Well—

JIM: You're going to be out of a job if you don't wake up.

TOM: I am waking up—

JIM: You show no signs.

TOM: The signs are interior.

[*Image on screen*: The sailing vessel with the Jolly Roger again.]

TOM: I'm planning to change. [*He leans over the fire-escape rail, speaking with quiet exhilaration. The incandescent marquees and signs of the first-run movie houses light his face from across the alley. He looks like a voyager.*] I'm right at the point of committing myself to a future that doesn't include the warehouse and Mr. Mendoza or even a night-school course in public speaking.

JIM: What are you gassing about?

TOM: I'm tired of the movies.

JIM: Movies!

TOM: Yes, movies! Look at them— [*a wave toward the marvels of Grand Avenue*] All of those glamorous people—having adventures—hogging it all, gobbling the whole thing up! You know what happens? People go to the *movies* instead of *moving!* Hollywood characters are supposed to have all the adventures for everybody in America, while everybody in America sits in a dark room and watches them have them! Yes, until there's a war. That's when adventure becomes available to the masses! *Everyone's* dish, not only Gable's! Then the people in the dark room come out of the dark room to have some adventures themselves—goody, goody! It's our turn now, to go to the South Sea Island—to make a safari—to be exotic, far-off! But I'm not patient. I don't want to wait till then. I'm tired of the *movies* and I am *about* to *move!*

JIM [*incredulously*]: Move?

TOM: Yes.

JIM: When?

TOM: Soon!

JIM: Where? Where?

[*The music seems to answer the question, while Tom thinks it over. He searches in his pockets.*]

TOM: I'm starting to boil inside. I know I seem dreamy, but inside—well, I'm boiling! Whenever I pick up a shoe, I shudder a little thinking how short life is and what I am doing! Whatever that means, I know it doesn't mean shoes—except as something to wear on a traveler's feet! [*He finds what he has been searching for in his pockets and holds out a paper to Jim.*] Look—

JIM: What?

TOM: I'm a member.

JIM [*reading*]: The Union of Merchant Seamen.

TOM: I paid my dues this month, instead of the light bill.

JIM: You will regret it when they turn the lights off.

TOM: I won't be here.

JIM: How about your mother?

TOM: I'm like my father. The bastard son of a bastard! Did you notice how he's grinning in his picture in there? And he's been absent going on sixteen years!

JIM: You're just talking, you drip. How does your mother feel about it?

TOM: Shhh! Here comes Mother! Mother is not acquainted with my plans!

AMANDA [*coming through the portieres*]: Where are you all?

TOM: On the terrace, Mother.

[*They start inside. She advances to them. Tom is distinctly shocked at her appearance. Even Jim blinks a little. He is making his first contact with girlish Southern vivacity and in spite of the night-school course in public speaking is somewhat thrown off the beam by the unexpected outlay of social charm. Certain responses are attempted by Jim but are swept aside by Amanda's gay laughter and chatter. Tom is embarrassed but after the first shock Jim reacts very warmly. He grins and chuckles, is altogether won over.*]

[*Image on screen*: Amanda as a girl.]

AMANDA [*coyly smiling, shaking her girlish ringlets*]: Well, well, well, so this is Mr. O'Connor. Introductions entirely unnecessary. I've heard so much about you from my boy. I finally said to him, Tom—good gracious!—why don't you bring this paragon to supper? I'd like to meet this nice young man at the warehouse!—instead of just hearing him sing your praises so much! I don't know why my son is so stand-offish—that's not Southern behavior!

Let's sit down and—I think we could stand a little more air in here! Tom, leave the door open. I felt a nice fresh breeze a moment ago. Where has it gone to? Mmm, so warm already! And not quite summer, even. We're going to burn up when summer really gets started. However, we're having—we're having a very light supper. I think light things are better fo' this time of year. The same as light clothes are. Light clothes an' light food are what warm weather calls fo'. You know our blood gets so thick during th' winter—it takes a while fo' us to *adjust* ou'selves!—when the season changes . . . It's come so quick this year. I wasn't prepared. All of a sudden—heavens! Already summer! I ran to the trunk an' pulled out this light dress—terribly old! Historical almost! But feels so good—so good an' co-ol, y' know. . . .

TOM: Mother—

AMANDA: Yes, honey?

TOM: How about—supper?

AMANDA: Honey, you go ask Sister if supper is ready! You know that Sister is in full charge of supper! Tell her you hungry boys are waiting for it. [*to Jim*] Have you met Laura?

JIM: She—

AMANDA: Let you in? Oh, good, you've met already! It's rare for a girl as sweet an' pretty as Laura to be domestic! But Laura is, thank heavens, not only pretty but also very domestic. I'm not at all. I never was a bit. I never could make a thing but angel-food cake. Well, in the South we had so many servants. Gone, gone, gone. All vestige of gracious living! Gone completely! I wasn't prepared for what the future brought me. All of my gentlemen callers were sons of planters and so of course I assumed that I would be married to one and raise my family on a large piece of land with plenty of servants. But man proposes—and woman accepts the proposal! To vary that old, old saying a little bit—I married no planter! I married a man who worked for the telephone company! That gallantly smiling gentleman over there! [*She points to the picture.*] A telephone man who—fell in love with long-distance! Now he travels and I don't even know where! But what am I going on for about my—tribulations? Tell me yours—I hope you don't have any! Tom?

TOM [*returning*]: Yes, Mother?

AMANDA: Is supper nearly ready?

TOM: It looks to me like supper is on the table.

AMANDA: Let me look— [*She rises prettily and looks through the portieres.*] Oh, lovely! But where is Sister?

TOM: Laura is not feeling well and she says that she thinks she'd better not come to the table.

AMANDA: What? Nonsense! Laura? Oh, Laura!

LAURA [*from the kitchenette, faintly*]: Yes, Mother.

AMANDA: You really must come to the table. We won't be seated until you come to the table! Come in, Mr. O'Connor. You sit over there, and I'll. . . . Laura? Laura Wingfield! You're keeping us waiting, honey! We can't say grace until you come to the table!

[*The kitchenette door is pushed weakly open and Laura comes in. She is obviously quite faint, her lips trembling, her eyes wide and staring. She moves unsteadily toward the table.*]

[*Screen legend*: "Terror!"]

[*Outside a summer storm is coming on abruptly. The white curtains billow inward at the windows and there is a sorrowful murmur from the deep blue dusk.*]

[*Laura suddenly stumbles; she catches at a chair with a faint moan.*]

TOM: Laura!

AMANDA: Laura!

[*There is a clap of thunder.*]

[*Screen legend*: "Ah!"]

[*despairingly*] Why, Laura, you *are* ill, darling! Tom, help your sister into the living room, dear! Sit in the living room, Laura—rest on the sofa. Well! [*to Jim as Tom helps his sister to the sofa in the living room*] Standing over the hot stove made her ill! I told her that it was just too warm this evening, but—

[*Tom comes back to the table.*]

Is Laura all right now?

TOM: Yes.

AMANDA: What *is* that? Rain? A nice cool rain has come up! [*She gives Jim a frightened look.*] I think we may—have grace—now . . .

[*Tom looks at her stupidly.*] Tom, honey—you say grace!

TOM: Oh . . . "For these and all thy mercies—"

[*They bow their heads, Amanda stealing a nervous glance at Jim. In the living room Laura, stretched on the sofa, clenches her hand to her lips, to hold back a shuddering sob.*]

God's Holy Name be praised—

[*The scene dims out.*]

SCENE SEVEN

It is half an hour later. Dinner is just being finished in the dining room, Laura is still huddled upon the sofa, her feet drawn under her, her head resting on a pale blue pillow, her eyes wide and mysteriously watchful. The new floor lamp with its shade of rose-colored silk gives a soft, becoming light to her face, bringing out the fragile, unearthly prettiness which usually escapes attention. From outside there is a steady murmur of rain, but it is slackening and soon stops; the air outside becomes pale and luminous as the moon breaks through the clouds. A moment after the curtain rises, the lights in both rooms flicker and go out.

JIM: Hey, there, Mr. Light Bulb!

[*Amanda laughs nervously.*]

[*Legend on screen*: "Suspension of a public service."]

AMANDA: Where was Moses when the lights went out? Ha-ha. Do you know the answer to that one, Mr. O'Connor?

JIM: No, Ma'am, what's the answer?

AMANDA: In the dark!

[*Jim laughs appreciatively.*]

Everybody sit still. I'll light the candles. Isn't it lucky we have them on the table? Where's a match? Which of you gentlemen can provide a match?

JIM: Here.

AMANDA: Thank you, Sir.

JIM: Not at all, Ma'am!

AMANDA [*as she lights the candles*]: I guess the fuse has burnt out. Mr. O'Connor, can you tell a burnt-out fuse? I know I can't and Tom is a total loss when it comes to mechanics.

[*They rise from the table and go into the kitchenette, from where their voices are heard.*]

Oh, be careful you don't bump into something. We don't want our gentleman caller to break his neck. Now wouldn't that be a fine howdy-do?

JIM: Ha-ha! Where is the fuse-box?

AMANDA: Right here next to the stove. Can you see anything?

JIM: Just a minute.

AMANDA: Isn't electricity a mysterious thing? Wasn't it Benjamin Franklin who tied a key to a kite? We live in such a mysterious universe, don't we? Some people say that science clears up all the mysteries for us. In my opinion it only creates more! Have you found it yet?

JIM: No, Ma'am. All these fuses look okay to me.

AMANDA: Tom!

TOM: Yes, Mother?

AMANDA: That light bill I gave you several days ago. The one I told you we got the notices about?

[*Legend on screen*: "Ha!"]

TOM: Oh—yeah.

AMANDA: You didn't neglect to pay it by any chance?

TOM: Why, I—

AMANDA: Didn't! I might have known it!

JIM: Shakespeare probably wrote a poem on that light bill, Mrs. Wingfield.

AMANDA: I might have known better than to trust him with it! There's such a high price for negligence in this world!

JIM: Maybe the poem will win a ten-dollar prize.

AMANDA: We'll just have to spend the remainder of the evening in the nineteenth century, before Mr. Edison made the Mazda lamp!

JIM: Candlelight is my favorite kind of light.

AMANDA: That shows you're romantic! But that's no excuse for Tom. Well, we got through dinner. Very considerate of them to let us get through dinner before they plunged us into everlasting darkness, wasn't it, Mr. O'Connor?

JIM: Ha-ha!

AMANDA: Tom, as a penalty for your carelessness you can help me with the dishes.

JIM: Let me give you a hand.

AMANDA: Indeed you will not!

JIM: I ought to be good for something.

AMANDA: Good for something? [*Her tone is rhapsodic.*] *You?* Why, Mr. O'Connor, nobody, *nobody's* given me this much entertainment in years—as you have!

JIM: Aw, now, Mrs. Wingfield!

AMANDA: I'm not exaggerating, not one bit! But Sister is all by her lonesome. You go keep her company in the parlor! I'll give you this lovely old candelabrum that used to be on the altar at the Church of the Heavenly Rest. It was melted a little out of shape when the church burnt down. Lightning struck it one spring. Gypsy Jones was holding a revival at the time and he intimated that the church was destroyed because the Episcopalians gave card parties.

JIM: Ha-ha.

AMANDA: And how about you coaxing Sister to drink a little wine? I think it would be good for her! Can you carry both at once?

JIM: Sure. I'm Superman!

AMANDA: Now, Thomas, get into this apron!

[*Jim comes into the dining room, carrying the candelabrum, its candles lighted, in one hand and a glass of wine in the other. The door of the kitchenette swings closed on Amanda's gay laughter; the flickering light approaches the portieres. Laura sits up nervously as Jim enters. She can hardly speak from the almost intolerable strain of being alone with a stranger.*]

[*Screen legend*: "I don't suppose you remember me at all!"]

[*At first, before Jim's warmth overcomes her paralyzing shyness, Laura's voice is thin and breathless, as though she had just run up a steep flight of stairs. Jim's attitude is gently humorous. While the incident is apparently unimportant, it is to Laura the climax of her secret life.*]

JIM: Hello there, Laura.

LAURA [*faintly*]: Hello.

[*She clears her throat.*]

JIM: How are you feeling now? Better?

LAURA: Yes. Yes, thank you.

JIM: This is for you. A little dandelion wine. [*He extends the glass toward her with extravagant gallantry.*]

LAURA: Thank you.

JIM: Drink it—but don't get drunk!

[*He laughs heartily. Laura takes the glass uncertainly; she laughs shyly.*]

Where shall I set the candles?

LAURA: Oh—oh, anywhere . . .

JIM: How about here on the floor? Any objections?

LAURA: No.

JIM: I'll spread a newspaper under to catch the drippings. I like to sit on the floor. Mind if I do?

LAURA: Oh, no.

JIM: Give me a pillow?

LAURA: What?

JIM: A pillow!

LAURA: Oh . . . [*She hands him one quickly.*]

JIM: How about you? Don't you like to sit on the floor?

LAURA: Oh—yes.

JIM: Why don't you, then?

LAURA: I—will.

JIM: Take a pillow!

[*Laura does. She sits on the floor on the other side of the candelabrum. Jim crosses his legs and smiles engagingly at her.*] I can't hardly see you sitting way over there.

LAURA: I can—see you.

JIM: I know, but that's not fair, I'm in the limelight.

[*Laura moves her pillow closer.*]

Good! Now I can see you! Comfortable?

LAURA: Yes.

JIM: So am I. Comfortable as a cow! Will you have some gum?

LAURA: No, thank you.

JIM: I think that I will indulge, with your permission. [*He musingly unwraps a stick of gum and holds it up.*] Think of the fortune made by the guy that invented the first piece of chewing gum. Amazing, huh? The Wrigley Building is one of the sights of Chicago—I saw it when I went up to the Century of Progress. Did you take in the Century of Progress?

LAURA: No, I didn't.

JIM: Well, it was quite a wonderful exposition. What impressed me most was the Hall of Science. Gives you an idea of what the future will be in America, even more wonderful than the present time is! [*There is a pause. Jim smiles at her.*] Your brother tells me you're shy. Is that right, Laura?

LAURA: I—don't know.

JIM: I judge you to be an old-fashioned type of girl. Well, I think that's a pretty good type to be. Hope you don't think I'm being too personal—do you?

LAURA [*hastily, out of embarrassment*]: I believe I *will* take a piece of gum, if you—don't mind. [*clearing her throat*] Mr. O'Connor, have you—kept up with your singing?

JIM: Singing? Me?

LAURA: Yes. I remember what a beautiful voice you had.

JIM: When did you hear me sing?

[*Laura does not answer, and in the long pause which follows a man's voice is heard singing offstage.*]

VOICE:

O blow, ye winds, heigh-ho,
A-roving I will go!
I'm off to my love
With a boxing glove—
Ten thousand miles away!

JIM: You say you've heard me sing?

LAURA: Oh, yes! Yes, very often . . . I—don't suppose—you remember me—at all?

JIM [*smiling doubtfully*]: You know I have an idea I've seen you before. I had that idea soon as you opened the door. It seemed almost like I was about to remember your name. But the name that I started to call you—wasn't a name! And so I stopped myself before I said it.

LAURA: Wasn't it—Blue Roses?

JIM [*springing up, grinning*]: Blue Roses! My gosh, yes—Blue Roses! That's what I had on my tongue when you opened the door! Isn't it funny what tricks your memory plays? I didn't connect you with high school somehow or other. But that's where it was; it was high school. I didn't even know you were Shakespeare's sister! Gosh, I'm sorry.

LAURA: I didn't expect you to. You—barely knew me!

JIM: But we did have a speaking acquaintance, huh?

LAURA: Yes, we—spoke to each other.

JIM: When did you recognize me?

LAURA: Oh, right away!

JIM: Soon as I came in the door?

LAURA: When I heard your name I thought it was probably you. I knew that Tom used to know you a little in high school. So when you came in the door—well, then I was—sure.

JIM: Why didn't you *say* something, then?

LAURA [*breathlessly*]: I didn't know what to say, I was —too surprised!

JIM: For goodness' sakes! You know, this sure is funny!

LAURA: Yes! Yes, isn't it, though . . .

JIM: Didn't we have a class in something together?

LAURA: Yes, we did.

JIM: What class was that?

LAURA: It was—singing—chorus!

JIM: Aw!

LAURA: I sat across the aisle from you in the Aud.

JIM: Aw.

LAURA: Mondays, Wednesdays, and Fridays.

JIM: Now I remember—you always came in late.

LAURA: Yes, it was so hard for me, getting upstairs. I had that brace on my leg—it clumped so loud!

JIM: I never heard any clumping.

LAURA [*wincing at the recollection*]: To me it sounded like—thunder!

JIM: Well, well, well, I never even noticed.

LAURA: And everybody was seated before I came in. I had to walk in front of all those people. My seat was in the back row. I had to go clumping all the way up the aisle with everyone watching!

JIM: You shouldn't have been self-conscious.

LAURA: I know, but I was. It was always such a relief when the singing started.

JIM: Aw, yes, I've placed you now! I used to call you Blue Roses. How was it that I got started calling you that?

LAURA: I was out of school a little while with pleurosis. When I came back you asked me what was the matter. I said I had pleurosis—you thought I said *Blue Roses*. That's what you always called me after that!

JIM: I hope you didn't mind.

LAURA: Oh, no—I liked it. You see, I wasn't acquainted with many—people. . . .

JIM: As I remember you sort of stuck by yourself.

LAURA: I—I—never have had much luck at—making friends.

JIM: I don't see why you wouldn't.

LAURA: Well, I—started out badly.

JIM: You mean being—

LAURA: Yes, it sort of—stood between me—

JIM: You shouldn't have let it!

LAURA: I know, but it did, and—

JIM: You were shy with people!

LAURA: I tried not to be but never could—

JIM: Overcome it?

LAURA: No, I—I never could!

JIM: I guess being shy is something you have to work out of kind of gradually.

LAURA [*sorrowfully*]: Yes—I guess it—

JIM: Takes time!

LAURA: Yes—

JIM: People are not so dreadful when you know them. That's what you have to remember! And everybody has problems, not just you, but practically everybody has got some problems. You think of yourself as having the only problems, as being the only one who is disappointed. But just look around you and you will see lots of people as disappointed as you are. For instance, I hoped when I was going to high school that I would be further along at this time, six years later, than I am now. You remember that wonderful write-up I had in *The Torch?*

LAURA: Yes! [*She rises and crosses to the table.*]

JIM: It said I was bound to succeed in anything I went into!

[*Laura returns with the high school yearbook.*]

Holy Jeez! *The Torch!*

[*He accepts it reverently. They smile across the book with mutual wonder. Laura crouches beside him and they begin to turn the pages. Laura's shyness is dissolving in his warmth.*]

LAURA: Here you are in *The Pirates of Penzance!*

JIM [*wistfully*]: I sang the baritone lead in that operetta.

LAURA [*raptly*]: So—*beautifully!*

JIM [*protesting*]: Aw—

LAURA: Yes, yes—beautifully—beautifully!

JIM: You heard me?

LAURA: All three times!

JIM: No!

LAURA: Yes!

JIM: All three performances?

LAURA [*looking down*]: Yes.

JIM: Why?

LAURA: I—wanted to ask you to—autograph my program. [*She takes the program from the back of the yearbook and shows it to him.*]

JIM: Why didn't you ask me to?

LAURA: You were always surrounded by your own friends so much that I never had a chance to.

JIM: You should have just—

LAURA: Well, I—thought you might think I was—

JIM: Thought I might think you was—what?

LAURA: Oh—

JIM [*with reflective relish*]: I was beleaguered by females in those days.

LAURA: You were terribly popular!

JIM: Yeah—

LAURA: You had such a—friendly way—

JIM: I was spoiled in high school.

LAURA: Everybody—liked you!

JIM: Including you?

LAURA: I—yes, I—did, too— [*She gently closes the book in her lap.*]

JIM: Well, well, well! Give me that program, Laura.

[*She hands it to him. He signs it with a flourish.*]

There you are—better late than never!

LAURA: Oh, I—what a—surprise!

JIM: My signature isn't worth very much right now. But some day—maybe—it will increase in value! Being disappointed is one thing and being discouraged is something else. I am disappointed but I am not discouraged. I'm twenty-three years old. How old are you?

LAURA: I'll be twenty-four in June.

JIM: That's not old age!

LAURA: No, but—

JIM: You finished high school?

LAURA [*with difficulty*]: I didn't go back.

JIM: You mean you dropped out?

LAURA: I made bad grades in my final examinations. [*She rises and replaces the book and the program on the table. Her voice is strained.*] How is—Emily Meisenbach getting along?

JIM: Oh, that kraut-head!

LAURA: Why do you call her that?

JIM: That's what she was.

LAURA: You're not still—going with her?

JIM: I never see her.

LAURA: It said in the "Personal" section that you were—engaged!

JIM: I know, but I wasn't impressed by that—propaganda!

LAURA: It wasn't—the truth?

JIM: Only in Emily's optimistic opinion!

LAURA: Oh—

[*Legend*: "What have you done since high school?"]

[*Jim lights a cigarette and leans indolently back on his elbows smiling at Laura with a warmth and charm which lights her inwardly with altar candles. She remains by the table, picks up a piece from the glass menagerie collection, and turns it in her hands to cover her tumult.*]

JIM [*after several reflective puffs on his cigarette*]: What have you done since high school?

[*She seems not to hear him.*]

Huh?

[*Laura looks up.*]

I said what have you done since high school, Laura?

LAURA: Nothing much.

JIM: You must have been doing something these six long years.

LAURA: Yes.

JIM: Well, then, such as what?

LAURA: I took a business course at business college—

JIM: How did that work out?

LAURA: Well, not very—well—I had to drop out, it gave me—indigestion—

[*Jim laughs gently.*]

JIM: What are you doing now?

LAURA: I don't do anything—much. Oh, please don't think I sit around doing nothing! My glass collection takes up a good deal of time. Glass is something you have to take good care of.

JIM: What did you say—about glass?

LAURA: Collection I said—I have one— [*She clears her throat and turns away again, acutely shy.*]

JIM [*abruptly*]: You know what I judge to be the trouble with you? Inferiority complex! Know what that is? That's what they call it when someone low-rates himself! I understand it because I had it, too. Although my case was not so aggravated as yours seems to be. I had it until I took up public speaking, developed my voice, and learned that I had an aptitude for science. Before that time I never thought of myself as being outstanding in any way whatsoever! Now I've never made a regular study of it, but I have a friend who says I can analyze people better than doctors that make a profession of it. I don't claim that to be necessarily true, but I can sure guess a person's psychology, Laura! [*He takes out his gum.*] Excuse me, Laura. I always take it out when the flavor is gone. I'll use this scrap of paper to wrap it in. I know how it is to get it stuck on a shoe. [*He wraps the gum in paper and puts it in his pocket.*] Yep—that's what I judge to be your principal trouble. A lack of confidence in yourself as a person. You don't have the proper amount of faith in yourself. I'm basing that fact on a number of your remarks and also on certain observations I've made. For instance that clumping you thought was so awful in high school. You say that you even dreaded to walk into class. You see what you did? You dropped out of school, you gave up an education because of a clump, which as far as I know was practically non-existent! A little physical defect is what you have. Hardly noticeable even! Magnified thousands of times by imagination! You know what my strong advice to you is? Think of yourself as *superior* in some way!

LAURA: In what way would I think?

JIM: Why, man alive, Laura! Just look about you a little. What do you see? A world full of common people! All of 'em born and all of 'em going to die! Which of them has one-tenth of your good points! Or mine! Or anyone else's, as far as that goes—gosh! Everybody excels in some one thing. Some in many! [*He unconsciously glances at himself in the mirror.*] All you've got to do is discover in *what!* Take me, for instance. [*He adjusts his tie at the mirror.*] My interest happens to lie in electro-dynamics. I'm taking a course in radio engineering at night school, Laura, on top of a fairly responsible job at the warehouse. I'm taking that course and studying public speaking.

LAURA: Ohhhh.

JIM: Because I believe in the future of television! [*turning his back to her.*] I wish to be ready to go up right along with it. Therefore I'm planning to get in on the ground floor. In fact I've already made the right connections and all that remains is for the industry itself to get under way! Full steam —[*His eyes are starry.*] *Knowledge*—Zzzzzp! *Money*— Zzzzzzp!—*Power!* That's the cycle democracy is built on!

[*His attitude is convincingly dynamic. Laura stares at him, even her shyness eclipsed in her absolute wonder. He suddenly grins.*]

I guess you think I think a lot of myself!

LAURA: No—o-o-o, I—

JIM: Now how about you? Isn't there something you take more interest in than anything else?

LAURA: Well, I do—as I said—have my—glass collection—

[*A peal of girlish laughter rings from the kitchenette.*]

JIM: I'm not right sure I know what you're talking about. What kind of glass is it?

LAURA: Little articles of it, they're ornaments mostly! Most of them are little animals made out of glass, the tiniest little animals in the world. Mother calls them a glass menagerie! Here's an example of one, if you'd like to see it! This one is one of the oldest. It's nearly thirteen.

[*Music*: "The Glass Menagerie."]

[*He stretches out his hand.*]

Oh, be careful—if you breathe, it breaks!

JIM: I'd better not take it. I'm pretty clumsy with things.

LAURA: Go on, I trust you with him! [*She places the piece in his palm.*] There now—you're holding him gently! Hold him over the light, he loves the light! You see how the light shines through him?

JIM: It sure does shine!

LAURA: I shouldn't be partial, but he is my favorite one.

JIM: What kind of a thing is this one supposed to be?

LAURA: Haven't you noticed the single horn on his forehead?

JIM: A unicorn, huh?

LAURA: Mmmm-hmmm!

JIM: Unicorns—aren't they extinct in the modern world?

LAURA: I know!

JIM: Poor little fellow, he must feel sort of lonesome.

LAURA [*smiling*]: Well, if he does, he doesn't complain about it. He stays on a shelf with some horses that don't have horns and all of them seem to get along nicely together.

JIM: How do you know?

LAURA [*lightly*]: I haven't heard any arguments among them!

JIM [*grinning*]: No arguments, huh? Well, that's a pretty good sign! Where shall I set him?

LAURA: Put him on the table. They all like a change of scenery once in a while!

JIM: Well, well, well, well—[*He places the glass piece on the table, then raises his arms and stretches.*] Look how big my shadow is when I stretch!

LAURA: Oh, oh, yes—it stretches across the ceiling!

JIM [*crossing to the door*]: I think it's stopped raining. [*He opens the fire-escape door and the background music changes to a dance tune.*] Where does the music come from?

LAURA: From the Paradise Dance Hall across the alley.

JIM: How about cutting the rug a little, Miss Wingfield?

LAURA: Oh, I—

JIM: Or is your program filled up? Let me have a look at it. [*He grasps an imaginary card.*] Why, every dance is taken! I'll just have to scratch some out.

[*Waltz music*: "La Golondrina."]

Ahhh, a waltz! [*He executes some sweeping turns by himself, then holds his arms toward Laura.*]

LAURA [*breathlessly*]: I—can't dance!

JIM: There you go, that inferiority stuff!

LAURA: I've never danced in my life!

JIM: Come on, try!

LAURA: Oh, but I'd step on you!

JIM: I'm not made out of glass.

LAURA: How—how—how do we start?

JIM: Just leave it to me. You hold your arms out a little.

LAURA: Like this?

JIM [*taking her in his arms*]: A little bit higher. Right. Now don't tighten up, that's the main thing about it—relax.

LAURA [*laughing breathlessly*]: It's hard not to.

JIM: Okay.

LAURA: I'm afraid you can't budge me.

JIM: What do you bet I can't? [*He swings her into motion.*]

LAURA: Goodness, yes, you can!

JIM: Let yourself go, now, Laura, just let yourself go.

LAURA: I'm—

JIM: Come on!

LAURA:—trying!

JIM: Not so stiff—easy does it!

LAURA: I know but I'm—

JIM: Loosen th' backbone! There now, that's a lot better.

LAURA: Am I?

JIM: Lots, lots better! [*He moves her about the room in a clumsy waltz.*]

LAURA: Oh, my!

JIM: Ha-ha!

LAURA: Oh, my goodness!

JIM: Ha-ha-ha!

[*They suddenly bump into the table, and the glass piece on it falls to the floor. Jim stops the dance.*]

What did we hit on?

LAURA: Table.

JIM: Did something fall off it? I think—

LAURA: Yes.

JIM: I hope that it wasn't the little glass horse with the horn!

LAURA: Yes. [*She stoops to pick it up.*]

JIM: Aw, aw, aw. Is it broken?

LAURA: Now it is just like all the other horses.

JIM: It's lost its—

LAURA: Horn! It doesn't matter. Maybe it's a blessing in disguise.

JIM: You'll never forgive me. I bet that that was your favorite piece of glass.

LAURA: I don't have favorites much. It's no tragedy, Freckles. Glass breaks so easily. No matter how careful you are. The traffic jars the shelves and things fall off them.

JIM: Still I'm awfully sorry that I was the cause.

LAURA [*smiling*]: I'll just imagine he had an operation. The horn was removed to make him feel less—freakish!

[*They both laugh.*]

Now he will feel more at home with the other horses, the ones that don't have horns. . . .

JIM: Ha-ha, that's very funny! [*Suddenly he is serious.*] I'm glad to see that you have a sense of humor. You know

—you're—well—very different! Surprisingly different from anyone else I know! [*His voice becomes soft and hesitant with a genuine feeling.*] Do you mind me telling you that?

[*Laura is abashed beyond speech.*]

I mean it in a nice way—

[*Laura nods shyly, looking away.*]

You make me feel sort of—I don't know how to put it! I'm usually pretty good at expressing things, but—this is something that I don't know how to say!

[*Laura touches her throat and clears it—turns the broken unicorn in her hands. His voice becomes softer.*]

Has anyone ever told you that you were pretty?

[*There is a pause, and the music rises slightly. Laura looks up slowly, with wonder, and shakes her head.*]

Well, you are! In a very different way from anyone else. And all the nicer because of the difference, too.

[*His voice becomes low and husky. Laura turns away, nearly faint with the novelty of her emotions.*]

I wish that you were my sister. I'd teach you to have some confidence in yourself. The different people are not like other people, but being different is nothing to be ashamed of. Because other people are not such wonderful people. They're one hundred times one thousand. You're one times one! They walk all over the earth. You just stay here. They're common as—weeds, but—you—well, you're—*Blue Roses!*

[*Image on screen*: Blue Roses.]

[*The music changes.*]

LAURA: But blue is wrong for—roses. . . .

JIM: It's right for you! You're—pretty!

LAURA: In what respect am I pretty?

JIM: In all respects—believe me! Your eyes—your hair—are pretty! Your hands are pretty! [*He catches hold of her hand.*] You think I'm making this up because I'm invited to dinner and have to be nice. Oh, I could do that! I could put on an act for you, Laura, and say lots of things without being very sincere. But this time I am. I'm talking to you sincerely. I happened to notice you had this inferiority complex that keeps you from feeling comfortable with people. Somebody needs to build your confidence up and make you proud instead of shy and turning away and—blushing. Somebody—ought to—*kiss* you, Laura!

[*His hand slips slowly up her arm to her shoulder as the music swells tumultuously. He suddenly turns her about and kisses her on the lips. When he releases her, Laura sinks on the sofa with a bright, dazed look. Jim backs away and fishes in his pocket for a cigarette.*]

[*Legend on screen*: "A souvenir."]

Stumblejohn!

[*He lights the cigarette, avoiding her look. There is a peal of girlish laughter from Amanda in the kitchenette. Laura slowly raises and opens her hand. It still contains the little broken glass animal. She looks at it with a tender, bewildered expression.*]

Stumblejohn! I shouldn't have done that—that was way off the beam. You don't smoke, do you?

[*She looks up, smiling, not hearing the question. He sits beside her rather gingerly. She looks at him speechlessly—*

waiting. He coughs decorously and moves a little farther aside as he considers the situation and senses her feelings, dimly, with perturbation. He speaks gently.]

Would you—care for a—mint?

[*She doesn't seem to hear him but her look grows brighter even.*]

Peppermint? Life Saver? My pocket's a regular drugstore —wherever I go . . . . [*He pops a mint in his mouth. Then he gulps and decides to make a clean breast of it. He speaks slowly and gingerly.*] Laura, you know, if I had a sister like you, I'd do the same thing as Tom. I'd bring out fellows and —introduce her to them. The right type of boys—of a type to —appreciate her. Only—well—he made a mistake about me. Maybe I've got no call to be saying this. That may not have been the idea in having me over. But what if it was? There's nothing wrong about that. The only trouble is that in my case—I'm not in a situation to—do the right thing. I can't take down your number and say I'll phone. I can't call up next week and—ask for a date. I thought I had better explain the situation in case you—misunderstood it and—I hurt your feelings. . . .

[*There is a pause. Slowly, very slowly, Laura's look changes, her eyes returning slowly from his to the glass figure in her palm. Amanda utters another gay laugh in the kitchenette.*]

LAURA [*faintly*]: You—won't—call again?

JIM: No, Laura, I can't. [*He rises from the sofa.*] As I was just explaining, I've—got strings on me. Laura, I've—been going steady! I go out all the time with a girl named Betty. She's a home-girl like you, and Catholic, and Irish, and in a great many ways we—get along fine. I met her last summer on a moonlight boat trip up the river to Alton, on the *Majestic*. Well—right away from the start it was—love!

[*Legend*: Love!]

[*Laura sways slightly forward and grips the arm of the sofa. He fails to notice. now enrapt in his own comfortable being.*]

Being in love has made a new man of me!

[*Leaning stiffly forward, clutching the arm of the sofa, Laura struggles visibly with her storm. But Jim is oblivious; she is a long way off.*]

The power of love is really pretty tremendous! Love is something that—changes the whole world, Laura!

[*The storm abates a little and Laura leans back. He notices her again.*]

It happened that Betty's aunt took sick, she got a wire and had to go to Centralia. So Tom—when he asked me to dinner—I naturally just accepted the invitation, not knowing that you—that he—that I— [*He stops awkwardly.*] Huh—I'm a stumblejohn!

[*He flops back on the sofa. The holy candles on the altar of Laura's face have been snuffed out. There is a look of almost infinite desolation. Jim glances at her uneasily.*]

I wish that you would—say something.

[*She bites her lip which was trembling and then bravely smiles. She opens her hand again on the broken glass figure. Then she gently takes his hand and raises it level with her own. She carefully places the unicorn in the palm of his hand, then pushes his fingers closed upon it.*]

What are you—doing that for? You want me to have him? Laura?

[*She nods.*]

What for?

LAURA: A—souvenir . . . .

[*She rises unsteadily and crouches beside the Victrola to wind it up.*]

[*Legend on screen*: "Things have a way of turning out so badly!" *Or image*: "Gentleman caller waving goodbye—gaily."]

[*At this moment Amanda rushes brightly back into the living room. She bears a pitcher of fruit punch in an old-fashioned cut-glass pitcher, and a plate of macaroons. The plate has a gold border and poppies painted on it.*]

AMANDA: Well, well, well! Isn't the air delightful after the shower? I've made you children a little liquid refreshment.

[*She turns gaily to Jim.*] Jim, do you know that song about lemonade?

"Lemonade, lemonade
Made in the shade and stirred with a spade—
Good enough for any old maid!"

JIM [*uneasily*]: Ha-ha! No—I never heard it.

AMANDA: Why, Laura! You look so serious!

JIM: We were having a serious conversation.

AMANDA: Good! Now you're better acquainted!

JIM [*uncertainly*]: Ha-ha! Yes.

AMANDA: You modern young people are much more serious-minded than my generation. I was so gay as a girl!

JIM: You haven't changed, Mrs. Wingfield.

AMANDA: Tonight I'm rejuvenated! The gaiety of the occasion, Mr. O'Connor! [*She tosses her head with a peal of laughter, spilling some lemonade.*] Oooo! I'm baptizing myself!

JIM: Here—let me—

AMANDA [*setting the pitcher down*]: There now. I discovered we had some maraschino cherries. I dumped them in, juice and all!

JIM: You shouldn't have gone to that trouble, Mrs. Wingfield.

AMANDA: Trouble, trouble? Why, it was loads of fun! Didn't you hear me cutting up in the kitchen? I bet your ears were burning! I told Tom how outdone with him I was for keeping you to himself so long a time! He should have brought you over much, much sooner! Well, now that you've found your way, I want you to be a very frequent caller! Not just occasional but all the time. Oh, we're going to have a lot of gay times together! I see them coming! Mmm, just breathe that air! So fresh, and the moon's so pretty! I'll skip back out—I know where my place is when young folks are having a—serious conversation!

JIM: Oh, don't go out, Mrs. Wingfield. The fact of the matter is I've got to be going.

AMANDA: Going, now? You're joking! Why, it's only the shank of the evening, Mr. O'Connor!

JIM: Well, you know how it is.

AMANDA: You mean you're a young workingman and have to keep workingmen's hours. We'll let you off early tonight. But only on the condition that next time you stay later. What's the best night for you? Isn't Saturday night the best night for you workingmen?

JIM: I have a couple of time-clocks to punch, Mrs. Wingfield. One at morning, another one at night!

AMANDA: My, but you *are* ambitious! You work at night, too?

JIM: No, Ma'am, not work but—Betty!

[*He crosses deliberately to pick up his hat. The band at the Paradise Dance Hall goes into a tender waltz.*]

AMANDA: Betty? Betty? Who's—Betty!

[*There is an ominous cracking sound in the sky.*]

JIM: Oh, just a girl. The girl I go steady with!

[*He smiles charmingly. The sky falls.*]

[*Legend*: "The Sky Falls."]

AMANDA [*a long-drawn exhalation*]: Ohhhh . . . Is it a serious romance, Mr. O'Connor?

JIM: We're going to be married the second Sunday in June.

AMANDA: Ohhhh—how nice! Tom didn't mention that you were engaged to be married.

JIM: The cat's not out of the bag at the warehouse yet. You know how they are. They call you Romeo and stuff like that. [*He stops at the oval mirror to put on his hat. He carefully shapes the brim and the crown to give a discreetly dashing effect.*] It's been a wonderful evening, Mrs. Wingfield. I guess this is what they mean by Southern hospitality.

AMANDA: It really wasn't anything at all.

JIM: I hope it don't seem like I'm rushing off. But I promised Betty I'd pick her up at the Wabash depot, an' by the time I get my jalopy down there her train'll be in. Some women are pretty upset if you keep 'em waiting.

AMANDA: Yes, I know—the tyranny of women! [*She extends her hand.*] Goodbye, Mr. O'Connor. I wish you luck—and happiness—and success! All three of them, and so does Laura! Don't you, Laura?

LAURA: Yes!

JIM [*taking Laura's hand*]: Goodbye, Laura. I'm certainly going to treasure that souvenir. And don't you forget the good advice I gave you. [*He raises his voice to a cheery shout.*] So long, Shakespeare! Thanks again, ladies. Good night!

[*He grins and ducks jauntily out. Still bravely grimacing, Amanda closes the door on the gentleman caller. Then she turns back to the room with a puzzled expression. She and Laura don't dare to face each other. Laura crouches beside the Victrola to wind it.*]

AMANDA [*faintly*]: Things have a way of turning out so badly. I don't believe that I would play the Victrola. Well, well—well! Our gentleman caller was engaged to be married! [*She raises her voice.*] Tom!

TOM [*from the kitchenette*]: Yes, Mother?

AMANDA: Come in here a minute. I want to tell you something awfully funny.

TOM [*entering with a macaroon and a glass of the lemonade*]: Has the gentleman caller gotten away already?

AMANDA: The gentleman caller has made an early departure. What a wonderful joke you played on us!

TOM: How do you mean?

AMANDA: You didn't mention that he was engaged to be married.

TOM: Jim? Engaged?

AMANDA: That's what he just informed us.

TOM: I'll be jiggered! I didn't know about that.

AMANDA: That seems very peculiar.

TOM: What's peculiar about it?

AMANDA: Didn't you call him your best friend down at the warehouse?

TOM: He is, but how did I know?

AMANDA: It seems extremely peculiar that you wouldn't know your best friend was going to be married!

TOM: The warehouse is where I work, not where I know things about people!

AMANDA: You don't know things anywhere! You live in a dream; you manufacture illusions!

[*He crosses to the door.*]

Where are you going?

TOM: I'm going to the movies.

AMANDA: That's right, now that you've had us make such fools of ourselves. The effort, the preparations, all the expense! The new floor lamp, the rug, the clothes for Laura! All for what? To entertain some other girl's fiancé! Go to the movies, go! Don't think about us, a mother deserted, an unmarried sister who's crippled and has no job! Don't let anything interfere with your selfish pleasure! Just go, go, go—to the movies!

TOM: All right, I will! The more you shout about my selfishness to me the quicker I'll go, and I won't go to the movies!

AMANDA: Go, then! Go to the moon—you selfish dreamer!

[*Tom smashes his glass on the floor. He plunges out on the fire escape, slamming the door. Laura screams in fright. The dance-hall music becomes louder. Tom stands on the fire escape, gripping the rail. The moon breaks through the storm clouds, illuminating his face.*]

[*Legend on screen*: "And so goodbye . . ."]

[*Tom's closing speech is timed with what is happening inside the house. We see, as though through soundproof glass, that Amanda appears to be making a comforting speech to Laura, who is huddled upon the sofa. Now that we cannot hear the mother's speech, her silliness is gone and she has dignity and tragic beauty. Laura's hair hides her face until, at the end of the speech, she lifts her head to smile at her mother. Amanda's gestures are slow and graceful, almost dancelike, as she comforts her daughter. At the end of her speech she glances a moment at the father's picture—then withdraws through the portieres. At the close of Tom's speech, Laura blows out the candles, ending the play.*]

TOM: I didn't go to the moon, I went much further—for time is the longest distance between two places. Not long after that I was fired for writing a poem on the lid of a shoe-box. I left Saint Louis. I descended the steps of this fire escape for a last time and followed, from then on, in my father's footsteps, attempting to find in motion what was lost in space. I traveled around a great deal. The cities swept about me like dead leaves, leaves that were brightly colored but torn away from the branches. I would have stopped, but I was pursued by something. It always came upon me unawares, taking me altogether by surprise. Perhaps it was a familiar bit of music. Perhaps it was only a piece of transparent glass. Perhaps I am walking along a street at night, in some strange city, before I have found companions. I pass the lighted window of a shop where perfume is sold. The window is filled with pieces of colored glass, tiny transparent bottles in delicate colors, like bits of a shattered rainbow. Then all at once my sister touches my shoulder. I turn around and look into her eyes. Oh, Laura, Laura, I tried to leave you behind me, but I am more faithful than I intended to be! I reach for a cigarette, I cross the street, I run into the movies or a bar, I buy a drink, I speak to the nearest stranger—anything that can blow your candles out!

[*Laura bends over the candles.*]

For nowadays the world is lit by lightning! Blow out your candles, Laura—and so goodbye. . . .

[*She blows the candles out.*]

THE CATASTROPHE OF SUCCESS

[*This essay was first published in the* New York Times *and later reprinted in* Story.]

This winter marked the third anniversary of the Chicago opening of "The Glass Menagerie," an event that terminated one part of my life and began another about as different in all external circumstances as could well be imagined. I was snatched out of virtual oblivion and thrust into sudden prominence, and from the precarious tenancy of furnished rooms about the country I was removed to a suite in a first-class Manhattan hotel. My experience was not unique. Success has often come that abruptly into the lives of Americans. The Cinderella story is our favorite national myth, the cornerstone of the film industry if not of the Democracy itself. I have seen it enacted on the screen so often that I was now inclined to yawn at it, not with disbelief but with an attitude of Who Cares! Anyone with such beautiful teeth and hair as the screen protagonist of such a story was bound to have a good time one way or another, and you could bet your bottom dollar and all the tea in China that that one would not be caught dead or alive at any meeting involving a social conscience.

No, my experience was not exceptional, but neither was it quite ordinary, and if you are willing to accept the somewhat eclectic proposition that I had not been writing with such an experience in mind—and many people are not willing to believe that a playwright is interested in anything but popular success—there may be some point in comparing the two estates.

The sort of life that I had had previous to this popular

success was one that required endurance, a life of clawing and scratching along a sheer surface and holding on tight with raw fingers to every inch of rock higher than the one caught hold of before, but it was a good life because it was the sort of life for which the human organism is created.

I was not aware of how much vital energy had gone into this struggle until the struggle was removed. I was out on a level plateau with my arms still thrashing and my lungs still grabbing at air that no longer resisted. This was security at last.

I sat down and looked about me and was suddenly very depressed. I thought to myself, this is just a period of adjustment. Tomorrow morning I will wake up in this first-class hotel suite above the discreet hum of an East Side boulevard and I will appreciate its elegance and luxuriate in its comforts and know that I have arrived at our American plan of Olympus. Tomorrow morning when I look at the green satin sofa I will fall in love with it. It is only temporarily that the green satin looks like slime on stagnant water.

But in the morning the inoffensive little sofa looked more revolting than the night before and I was already getting too fat for the $125 suit which a fashionable acquaintance had selected for me. In the suite things began to break accidentally. An arm came off the sofa. Cigarette burns appeared on the polished surface of the furniture. Windows were left open and a rain storm flooded the suite. But the maid always put it straight and the patience of the management was inexhaustible. Late parties could not offend them seriously. Nothing short of a demolition bomb seemed to bother my neighbors.

I lived on room service. But in this, too, there was a disenchantment. Some time between the moment when I ordered dinner over the phone and when it was rolled into my living room like a corpse on a rubber-wheeled table, I lost all interest in it. Once I ordered a sirloin steak and a chocolate sundae, but everything was so cunningly disguised on the table that

I mistook the chocolate sauce for gravy and poured it over the sirloin steak.

Of course all this was the more trivial aspect of a spiritual dislocation that began to manifest itself in far more disturbing ways. I soon found myself becoming indifferent to people. A well of cynicism rose in me. Conversations all sounded as if they had been recorded years ago and were being played back on a turntable. Sincerity and kindliness seemed to have gone out of my friends' voices. I suspected them of hypocrisy. I stopped calling them, stopped seeing them. I was impatient of what I took to be inane flattery.

I got so sick of hearing people say, "I loved your play!" that I could not say thank you any more. I choked on the words and turned rudely away from the usually sincere person. I no longer felt any pride in the play itself but began to dislike it, probably because I felt too lifeless inside ever to create another. I was walking around dead in my shoes and I knew it but there were no friends I knew or trusted sufficiently, at that time, to take them aside and tell them what was the matter.

This curious condition persisted about three months, till late spring, when I decided to have another eye operation mainly because of the excuse it gave me to withdraw from the world behind a gauze mask. It was my fourth eye operation, and perhaps I should explain that I had been afflicted for about five years with a cataract on my left eye which required a series of needling operations and finally an operation on the muscle of the eye. (The eye is still in my head. So much for that.)

Well, the gauze mask served a purpose. While I was resting in the hospital the friends whom I had neglected or affronted in one way or another began to call on me and now that I was in pain and darkness, their voices seemed to have changed, or rather that unpleasant mutation which I had suspected earlier in the season had now disappeared and they sounded now as they had used to sound in the lamented days of my obscurity. Once more they were sincere and kindly voices with the ring of truth in them and that quality of understanding for which I had originally sought them out.

As far as my physical vision was concerned, this last operation was only relatively successful (although it left me with an apparently clear black pupil in the right position, or nearly so) but in another, figurative way, it had served a much deeper purpose.

When the gauze mask was removed I found myself in a readjusted world. I checked out of the handsome suite at the first-class hotel, packed my papers and a few incidental belongings and left for Mexico, an elemental country where you can quickly forget the false dignities and conceits imposed by success, a country where vagrants innocent as children curl up to sleep on the pavements and human voices, especially when their language is not familiar to the ear, are soft as birds'. My public self, that artifice of mirrors, did not exist here and so my natural being was resumed.

Then, as a final act of restoration, I settled for a while at Chapala to work on a play called "The Poker Night," which later became "A Streetcar Named Desire." It is only in his work that an artist can find reality and satisfaction, for the actual world is less intense than the world of his invention and consequently his life, without recourse to violent disorder, does not seem very substantial. The right condition for him is that in which his work is not only convenient but unavoidable.

For me a convenient place to work is a remote place among strangers where there is good swimming. But life should require a certain minimal effort. You should not have too many people waiting on you, you should have to do most things for yourself. Hotel service is embarrassing. Maids, waiters, bellhops, porters and so forth are the most embarrassing people in the world for they continually remind you of inequities which we accept as the proper thing. The sight of an ancient woman, gasping and wheezing as she drags a heavy pail of water down a hotel corridor to mop up the mess of some drunken overprivileged guest, is one that sickens and weighs upon the heart and withers it with shame for this world in which it is not only tolerated but regarded as proof positive that the wheels of Democracy are functioning as they should without interference from above or below. Nobody should have to clean up anybody else's mess in this world. It is terribly bad for both parties, but probably worse for the one receiving the service.

I have been corrupted as much as anyone else by the vast number of menial services which our society has grown to expect and depend on. We should do for ourselves or let the machines do for us, the glorious technology that is supposed to be the new light of the world. We are like a man who has bought a great amount of equipment for a camping trip, who has the canoe and the tent and the fishing lines and the axe and the guns, the mackinaw and the blankets, but who now, when all the preparations and the provisions are piled expertly together, is suddenly too timid to set out on the journey but remains where he was yesterday and the day before and the day before that, looking suspiciously through white lace curtains at the clear sky he distrusts. Our great technology is a God-given chance for adventure and for progress which we are afraid to attempt. Our ideas and our ideals remain exactly what they were and where they were three centuries ago. No. I beg your pardon. It is no longer safe for a man even to declare them!

This is a long excursion from a small theme into a large one which I did not intend to make, so let me go back to what I was saying before.

This is an oversimplification. One does not escape that

easily from the seduction of an effete way of life. You cannot arbitrarily say to yourself, I will now continue my life as it was before this thing, Success, happened to me. But once you fully apprehend the vacuity of a life without struggle you are equipped with the basic means of salvation. Once you know this is true, that the heart of man, his body and his brain, are forged in a white-hot furnace for the purpose of conflict (the struggle of creation) and that with the conflict removed, the man is a sword cutting daisies, that not privation but luxury is the wolf at the door and that the fangs of this wolf are all the little vanities and conceits and laxities that Success is heir to—why, then with this knowledge you are at least in a position of knowing where danger lies.

You know, then, that the public Somebody you are when you "have a name" is a fiction created with mirrors and that the only somebody worth being is the solitary and unseen you that existed from your first breath and which is the sum of your actions and so is constantly in a state of becoming under your own violation—and knowing these things, you can even survive the catastrophe of Success!

It is never altogether too late, unless you embrace the Bitch Goddess, as William James called her, with both arms and find in her smothering caresses exactly what the homesick little boy in you always wanted, absolute protection and utter effortlessness. Security is a kind of death, I think, and it can come to you in a storm of royalty checks beside a kidney-shaped pool in Beverly Hills or anywhere at all that is removed from the conditions that made you an artist, if that's what you are or were or intended to be. Ask anyone who has experienced the kind of success I am talking about— What good is it? Perhaps to get an honest answer you will have to give him a shot of truth serum but the word he will finally groan is unprintable in genteel publications.

Then what is good? The obsessive interest in human affairs,

plus a certain amount of compassion and moral conviction, that first made the experience of living something that must be translated into pigment or music or bodily movement or poetry or prose or anything that's dynamic and expressive—that's what's good for you if you're at all serious in your aims. William Saroyan wrote a great play on this theme, that purity of heart is the one success worth having. "In the time of your life—live!" That time is short and it doesn't return again. It is slipping away while I write this and while you read it, and the monosyllable of the clock is Loss, loss, loss, unless you devote your heart to its opposition.

Notes

(These notes are intended for use by foreign-language students as well as by English-speaking readers.)

3 *hive-like conglomerations . . .*: compares the cramped identical units of an apartment block to the cells of a beehive.
interfused mass of automatism . . .: suggests that the American lower-middle class has been trained to behave like robots, without individuality, and continues the idea of worker bees.
poetic license: the freedom to use poetic imagination.
garbage cans: dustbins.

4 *proscenium*: arch which surrounds stage in some theatres.
portieres: a curtain over door.
whatnot: a stand with shelves for knick-knacks.
doughboy: American infantryman.
Gregg shorthand diagram: chart indicating conventions for secretarial note-taking.

5 *Braille alphabet*: alphabet for the blind; system of raised dots which can be 'read' by the fingertips.
In Spain there was revolution . . .: refers to the revolt against the Republican government by the Fascist leader General Franco in 1936, which sparked the three-year-long Spanish Civil War.
Guernica: refers to the ruthless aerial bombardment of the town in April 1937 by German bombers

fighting for Franco.
emissary: messenger.
mantel: shelf over fireplace.
skipped the light fantastic: danced.

6 *'Ou sont les neiges'*: 'Where are the snows?' (French). Part of a well-known quotation *'Ou sont les neiges d'antan?'* ('Where are the snows of yesteryear?') from a poem by François Villon; an expression of nostalgia.
drop-leaf table: a table with a hinged flap which can be used to make it larger or dropped to take up less space.
scrim: gauze screen which becomes transparent when lit from behind.
mastication: chewing.

7 *Metropolitan star*: singer at the Metropolitan Opera.
blancmange: gelatine-based dessert.
darky: offensive term for African-American.
gentleman caller: term for suitor visiting a young lady in the Old South.

8 *nigger*: offensive term for African-American.
Parish house: church hall.
planters: owners of large cotton farms (plantations).
Mississippi Delta: region of the Deep South in which the Mississippi river broadens before flowing into the Gulf of Mexico.

9 *elegiac*: an elegy is a song of lamentation; Amanda looks nostalgically to the past.
Government bonds: investment certificates guaranteed by US government.
beaux: boyfriends.
Memphis: biggest city in the state of Tennessee.
Wall Street: New York City's financial district.

Midas touch: refers to the mythical King Midas, whose touch would turn objects to gold.

10 *in a fugitive manner*: as if running away.

old maid: spinster.

11 *cloche hats*: bell-shaped hats.

pocketbook: handbag.

D.A.R.: Daughters of the American Revolution: an organisation of respectable middle-class women.

13 *a swarm of typewriters*: a disorientating image of many typewriters; the phrase suggests them buzzing like bees.

Rubicam's Business College: further education college in St Louis, Missouri.

14 *Famous-Barr*: department store.

up the spout: disappearing like steam from a kettle.

Victrola: brand name of an early record player.

courting pneumonia: risking catching severe illness from the cold.

15 *The Crust of Humility*: phrase suggesting the scraps of dried bread given to beggars.

16 *phonograph*: early form of record player.

nervous indigestion: stomach pains resulting from stress.

occupy a position: take up a wage-earning occupation.

yearbook: annual high school publication detailing the achievements of that year's class members.

'The Pirates of Penzance': comic operetta by Gilbert and Sullivan.

17 *the Aud.*: high-school auditorium.

debating: competition in public speaking and rhetoric.

jolly disposition: a happy temperament.

pleurosis: disease involving inflammation of

membrane covering lungs.
Soldan: name of a high school in St Louis, Missouri.
Personal Section: part of newspaper dedicated to readers' announcements.
not cut out for: not designed for.
19 *fiasco*: ludicrous or humiliating failure.
archetype of the universal unconscious: refers to the psychological theories of C.G. Jung, who believed that the same basic character types recur in the dreams and mythologies of all human cultures, and represent aspects of underlying psychological needs.
specter: ghost.
feather the nest and plume the bird: provide money and beautiful clothing to make a daughter more attractive to potential suitors.
roping in subscribers: attracting regular customers for a journal.
matrons: mature married women.
serialized sublimations: refers to episodic magazine stories; 'sublimation' is a concept of psychologist Sigmund Freud, who believed that the human being's animal instincts for sex and pleasure are suppressed and so rechannelled (sublimated) into more 'respectable' forms by societal convention.
delicate cuplike breasts . . . (etc.): satirises politely restrained manner in which women's magazines of the period alluded to sex.
Etruscan sculpture: sculpture from early pre-Roman Italy.
glamor magazine: fashion magazine.
20 *sinus condition*: inflammation of the air passages between skull and nose.
Christian martyr: one who suffers for the faith.

'Gone with the Wind': episodic romantic novel of the American Civil War by Margaret Mitchell; made into blockbuster movie in 1939.
Scarlett O'Hara: heroine of *Gone with the Wind*.
post-World-War generation: those who came of age in the years directly after the First World War (1914–18).
hold the wire: stay on the telephone line.
hung up: cut off telephone communication.

21 *that insane Mr Lawrence*: refers to poet and novelist D.H. Lawrence, whose controversial books (such as *Lady Chatterley's Lover*) treated sex with unusual frankness and explicitness.

22 *gesticulating shadows*: suggests wild hand gestures and pointing from Amanda and Tom, being cast in shadow form on ceiling.

23 *moping, doping*: suggests Tom behaving as if miserable and exhausted.
celotex interior with fluorescent tubes: suggests claustrophobic working environment, with industrial wall cladding and no natural light.

24 *opium dens, dens of vice*, etc.: secret locations for illegal activities such as drug-taking.
tommy gun: light machine gun (invented by J. T. Thompson).
cat houses: brothels.
czar of the underworld: leader of organised crime ring.
whiskers: beard.
El Diablo: the Devil (Spanish).

26 *Garbo picture*: film starring Greta Garbo.
travelogue: documentary film about exotic journey.
newsreel: before the days of television news was shown in the cinema.

organ solo: many cinemas were still equipped with the organs which had accompanied silent films and these sometimes provided musical interludes.
Milk Fund: charitable organisation.

27 *pitchers*: jugs.
Kentucky Straight Bourbon: type of whisky.
two-by-four: standard size of strips of wood.

29 *Sticks and stones . . .* (etc.): Amanda's variation of the old proverb, 'Sticks and stones may break our bones, but words can never hurt us.'
gloomy gray vault of the areaway: dark, narrow passage between tall apartment buildings.
satirical as a Daumier print: refers to nineteenth-century French artist, Honoré Daumier, famed for satirical caricatures.

30 *Ave Maria*: Roman Catholic prayer to the Virgin Mary, often sung.
right-hand bower: 'a right bower' is the knave of trumps, a useful card in card games, possibly with connotations of being a bit of a rogue. Here the phrase also suggests a right-hand man or trusted deputy.

31 *natural endowments*: talents and abilities.
Purina; Shredded wheat: breakfast cereals.

32 *Spartan endurance*: ability to endure great difficulties or deprivation. In ancient Greece, the citizens of Sparta were famous for living lives of austere simplicity, without luxuries or comforts.

33 *inquisition*: intense questioning; interrogation.
Jolly Roger: flag of pirate ship, with image of skull and crossed bones.

34 *to punch in red*: to arrive late for work.

35 *handwriting on the wall*: a prophecy of future doom (Biblical reference).

Merchant Marine: Merchant Navy.
Young People's League: church-based social group.
36 *wool muffler*: scarf; neck-warmer.
37 *horsey set*: rich people who own horses.
Long Island: affluent suburb of New York City.
38 *Annunciation*: announcement (usually refers to the story of the Angel Gabriel telling the Virgin Mary of her pregnancy).
Franco: General Franco, leader of the Fascists in the Spanish Civil War.
39 *ash pits*: where ash from home fires was disposed of.
Berchtesgaden: country retreat of German dictator Adolf Hitler.
Chamberlain: British Prime Minister Neville Chamberlain; responsible for discredited policy of 'appeasing' Hitler by allowing him limited territorial expansion in Europe.
hot swing music: type of upbeat jazz.
40 *sphinx*: inscrutable creature of ancient Egypt; lion with a woman's head; spoke in riddles.
42 *putting on*: teasing.
43 *work like a Turk!*: work very hard.
chintz: cotton printed with coloured design.
Durkee's dressing: type of spiced dressing for fish.
44 *cowlick*: tuft of hair sticking up from head.
get-up: energy and initiative ('get-up-and-go').
46 *homely*: plain-looking, or perhaps rather ugly.
47 *eloquent as an oyster*: ironic epithet referring to Tom's frequent silences (i.e. his mouth is shut as tight as an oyster shell).
50 *senior class*: final-year high school students (17–18 years old).
glee club: singing group specialising in merry

songs.
White House: official home of the President of the United States.
51 *folks*: family.
52 *Gay Deceivers*: padding for brassière.
53 *Possess your soul in patience*: wait patiently.
voile: thin, semi-transparent material.
jonquils: flowers of narcissus family; similar to daffodils.
cotillion: in America, a formal coming-out ball for debutantes.
cakewalk: energetic dance competition from the Deep South (developed from African-American slaves or servants dancing wildly for a prize of a cake).
sashay: ostentatious, gliding walk aided by big skirts.
quinine: bitter medicine used for malaria.
54 *dogwood*: small tree with white flowers and purple berries.
57 *goings on*: activities; occurrences.
'Dardanella': popular tune.
58 *'Post Dispatch'*: *St Louis Post Dispatch*; local newspaper.
59 *Dizzy Dean*: famous baseball player.
sell you a bill of goods: Jim is saying he will try to persuade Tom to 'buy into' an idea he is 'selling'.
executive positions: jobs with managerial status within corporations.
helluva lot: 'hell of a lot'; a very great deal.
60 *incandescent marquees and signs*: the brightly-lit advertising hoardings above and outside theatres, etc.
first-run movie houses: cinemas where films appear

first before general release.
61 *gassing*: talking emptily ('hot air').
hogging it all: selfishly holding on to everything.
dark room: interior of cinema.
Gable: Clark Gable, the movie star.
62 *Union of Merchant Seamen*: trade union for sailors.
63 *stand-offish*: distant; unfriendly.
64 *angel-food cake*: simple cake made of flour, sugar and egg-whites.
68 *howdy-do*: bothersome business.
Benjamin Franklin: American statesman (1706–90), also famous for his scientific experiments and the invention of the lightning conductor referred to here.
69 *Mr Edison*: Thomas Edison, inventor of the electric light bulb.
Mazda lamp: brand of electric lamp.
70 *Gypsy Jones*: famous evangelist.
72 *Wrigley Building*: headquarters of Wrigley's chewing-gum corporation.
Century of Progress: large exposition in Chicago celebrating American achievements of nineteenth and twentieth centuries.
75 *clumping*: suggests the dull, hollow sound made by a braced or wooden leg when it makes contact with floor.
76 *'The Torch'*: title of Soldan High School's yearbook.
78 *beleaguered*: constantly pestered by; weighed down by.
79 *kraut-head*: derogatory term for person of German descent.
80 *inferiority complex*: psychoanalytic term for person who thinks of him- or herself as insignificant,

inferior to others.

82 *electro-dynamics*: study of electricity in motion, or of the interaction of electric currents.

83 *unicorn*: mythical, horse-like creature with single horn on its forehead.

84 *cutting the rug*: dancing.

is your program filled?: at a ball a gentleman would book a dance with a lady in advance and his name would be written on her dance-card or programme.

88 *Stumblejohn*: clumsy, awkward person.

89 *Life Savers*: brand of American peppermints.

drugstore: chemist's shop, usually selling a variety of goods including refreshments.

90 *Alton*: town in Illinois just up the Mississippi from St Louis.

Centralia: Missouri town over 100 miles west of St Louis.

91 *macaroons*: sweet biscuits made of almonds.

92 *maraschino cherries*: cherries preserved in liqueur, used for decorating cocktails.

outdone with him: peeved or miffed.

it's only the shank of the evening: the night is young.

93 *go steady with*: have longstanding relationship with.

cat's not out of the bag: secret has not been revealed.

94 *Wabash depot*: train station on Wabash Avenue.

jalopy: dilapidated motor car.

95 *I'll be jiggered!*: expression of astonishment.

97 *the world is lit by lightning*: refers poetically to the brash modern era of bright lights and noise, in which Laura's extreme delicacy is helplessly out of place.

Questions for Further Study

1 Whom do you regard as the central character in this play, and why? In developing your argument, make sure you consider possible reasons why other characters might or might not also be seen as central.
2 In what ways do Amanda's rose-tinted memories of her past impact on her hopes for her family's future? And do those hopes impact positively or negatively on her children's present well-being?
3 Choose a scene in which Laura's silences seem to you particularly acute. Provide an analysis of the scene's 'subtext' by explaining what you think she is thinking and feeling in her quietness. How might this subtext best be brought out in a performance of the scene?
4 In what ways to we see Tom struggling with his conscience during the play, and to what extent are we encouraged to sympathise with him in his struggle? Does the presence in the play of the 'older' Tom, as narrator, mean that we see the younger Tom's anxieties in a different light than we might otherwise?
5 Why do you think Tom describes Jim as 'the most realistic character in the play'? To what extent does Jim's 'realism' suggest a contrast to the 'idealism' or 'romanticism' of the other characters?
6 Consider the significance of the absent father figure to the action of the play. In what ways does

Williams succeed in rendering this absence as a kind of ghostly presence?

7 *The Glass Menagerie* is presented by Tom as a 'memory play' about his own past. How important is this framing of the play's events as memory to our understanding of the action? (Would it matter if Tom's monologues were cut?)

8 Consider how differently the play's events would be presented if we were to see them from the point of view of one of the other characters, instead of Tom. You should consider whether the play's key dramatic moments might be 'remembered' differently, but make sure you also think about such elements as scene structure, and the choice of which events are significant to show on stage in the first place (rather than just describe in narration).

9 Why do you think Williams divided the play into seven 'scenes' of such irregular lengths, rather than using longer 'acts' (two, three or four) of more even length, as was the convention at the time? (It might help to contrast the play with a more conventional piece of the same period, such as Arthur Miller's *All My Sons*.)

10 What does an awareness of Tennessee Williams's personal family history add to an understanding of *The Glass Menagerie*? What are the possible advantages or drawbacks of viewing the play in this light?

11 What role does the idea of 'the South' play in *The Glass Menagerie*, given that it is set in St Louis Missouri (which is a Southern state, but not in 'the deep South')? How might an understanding of the history of America's north/south divide aid an understanding of the play?

12 Williams carefully sets the play's action in 1938, during the Spanish Civil War, and on the verge of the Second World War. How significant is this historical location to an understanding of the play's action?

13 Williams insisted that *The Glass Menagerie* is not 'a straight realistic play with its genuine Frigidaire and authentic ice-cubes', and in the opening monologue, Tom also stresses that 'it is not realistic'. What is meant by the term 'realism' in drama, and to what extent do you think this play resists or questions the 'rules' of realism?

14 How is Williams's notion of 'sculptural drama' (see commentary, p. lxiii) realised through his stage directions for the play? Consider some of the ways in which this sculptural quality is made apparent in particular scenes or moments in the play, and discuss the ways in which you think it relates to or enhances the play's narrative.

15 If you were to direct a production of *The Glass Menagerie*, would you seek to follow or to disregard Williams's suggestions for the projection of images and titles to accompany the stage action? Give reasons for your choice, using specific examples to support it.

16 Analyse Williams's decision to set the whole play in a single, cramped apartment. What 'role' does this setting play in the action of the play, and in the light of your analysis, what are the most important considerations for a set designer working on the play?

17 Choose two characters in the play, and discuss the moment(s) in the action when you think they display the most tenderness towards each other.

Contrast this with discussion of moments in which there is particular tension or hostility between them. What do these contrasts tell us about the characters' relationship?

18 Choose one or two of the play's characters, and analyse the ways in which they can be seen, on occasion, to be 'play-acting' or 'performing a role' for the benefit of other characters. Consider some of the contrasting motives (conscious or unconscious) underlying such role play, and the degrees of deception (or self-deception) involved.

19 Consider the extent to which any one or two of the play's characters can be seen to be avoiding or hiding from the truth of their situation(s). To what extent are we encouraged to sympathise with, or to criticse, this self-deception?

20 Look in detail at the long dialogue between Jim and Laura in Scene Seven. Analyse the emotional journeys on which both characters go during the course of this almost static scene, considering the (possibly differing) ways in which each understands the significance of particular moments. In the light of your analysis, what would be the key advice you would give to actors performing the scene?

21 Do you see the play, ultimately, as a tragedy or a kind of bittersweet comedy? Be sure to research the meaning of these terms, and to explain your reasoning carefully.

22 Williams is often credited with initiating what became known as 'the American style' of post-war drama, thanks to the way that plays like *The Glass Menagerie* and *A Streetcar Named Desire* blend aspects of domestic realism with more fluid states suggesting dream or memory. Consider some of the

ways in which Williams established this 'style' in *Menagerie*, and compare and contrast his approach to that of Arthur Miller in *Death of a Salesman* (another prime case of 'the American style').

STEPHEN BOTTOMS is the Wole Soyinka Professor of Drama and Theatre Studies at the University of Leeds. He taught previously at the University of Glasgow from 1993 to 2005. A specialist in contemporary American theatre, he is the author of *The Theatre of Sam Shepard* (Cambridge University Press, 1998), *Albee: Who's Afraid of Virginia Woolf?* (CUP 2000), *Playing Underground: A Critical History of the 1960s Off-Off-Broadway Movement'* (University of Michigan Press, 2004), and editor of *The Cambridge Companion to Edward Albee* (2005). He also regularly directs for the stage: his own production of *The Glass Menagerie* for Flexible Deadlock Theatre Company toured in Scotland in 1999.